THE YOGA LAW BOOK

Legal Essentials For Yoga Professionals

CORY SCOTT DANKNER STERLING, J.D

Published by Conscious Counsel Legal Services, March, 2019

ISBN: 9781999039608

Editor: Aruna Dahanayake
Typeset: Greg Salisbury
Portrait Photographer: Darko Sikman
Yogi Model on Cover: Kate Gillespie

READ THIS FIRST: A Legal Disclaimer

Dearest yogis and passionate heart-leading entrepreneurs who may pick up this book:

Before we start the party and learn just how FUN law can be, I need to be really clear about something. The information contained in this book is not legal advice, and even though you are reading this book (which is super rad) I am not formally your lawyer.

In order for me to be your lawyer (I would love to be, by the way), you would have to officially sign up as a client of Conscious Counsel, and *only then* would I be giving you legal advice.

What is written in this book is my understanding of the law and how it applies to yoga professionals – it isn't the law itself. I graduated law school with first-class honours and have been a member in good standing with the British Columbia Law Society since 2015. With that being said, I may share opinions in this book that in fact do not reflect best legal practices. They are *my ideas as an individual and entrepreneur and someone who has seen the same legal challenges stand in front of yoga professionals over and over again.*

Further, I have written this book to explain general legal principles. This means that I have not included *all* of the information on the topics discussed (that would make it a law text book) and instead I have chosen what I think is most likely to apply to yoga professionals. This also means that I have not written a book which applies to any specific jurisdiction. I practice as a lawyer in Canada but I have never studied American, Australian or European law. That being said, I have spoken with lawyers in various jurisdictions and generally speaking, I have received the thumbs-up.

I have included many stories in this book that have actually happened to my clients. The purpose of including their stories is so that you can see what mistakes they made, learn from them and then not make the same mistakes yourself. In almost all instances (save Ashley Boone in the last two chapters), the names of the people in the stories have been changed and the specifics of their yoga business have been altered to avoid anyone being able to identify them by virtue of the information in the story. All of the stories happened, but not precisely in the way I am sharing them with you – hence the word 'story'.

My intention in writing this book is for you to learn about the law in an approachable and FUN way. The intention is not for this book to serve as your lawyer or explain everything you'll ever need to know about the law.

So, in continuing to use this book, you acknowledge that this book is not legal advice and that you will not take it to be such. You also acknowledge that you will be solely responsible for any actions you take based on this book relating to the law or your business. If you need legal help, please connect with Conscious Counsel or reach out to a lawyer in your jurisdiction.

Again, THE CONTENT IN THIS BOOK IS NOT LEGAL ADVICE. I'M JUST TRYING TO TURN YOUR MIND TO IMPORTANT LEGAL PRINCIPLES AND SHARE STORIES THAT I HAVE GONE THROUGH AND EXPERIENCED WITH MY CLIENTS SO YOU CAN AVOID ANY SUCH PROBLEMS.

All of this being said, the book you are holding was written with love, tons of research and lots of hard work. So, I hope you enjoy!

This book is dedicated to my parents who have provided me with the unconditional love and continuous support which has made me the person I am today. Thank you.

CONTENTS

Disclaimer III

Dedication V

Introduction: Why Yoga Law? IX

1. The New Legal Paradigm 1

2. Why Everyone Hates Lawyers But Really Shouldn't.......13

3. Why it's a Bad Idea to Download Contracts from the Internet........33

4. Choosing Your Posture: Corporate Structures + Setting Up Your Business 59

5. Waivers and Insurance Are A Real Thing............................87

6. Pay Attention: The Difference Between Independent Contractors + Employees...111

7. Building Your Yogi Brand, Protecting Your Yogi Assets 131

8. Yogis Operating Online 161

9. Putting It All Together: Building Muskoka Yoga Festival.............177

10. Savasana: Lessons + Results from Muskoka Yoga Festival...........211

About the Author...225

More About the Author...226

Introduction: Why Yoga Law?

Why am I writing this book? I have been writing for pleasure for years and always knew that my efforts would culminate in a book, but I never thought it would be a book about Yoga Law.

The first and most important reason why I am writing this book is that yoga, as I understand it, is about serving others. I feel that sharing the information in this book is an act of service. When I completed my yoga teacher training and began organizing my endless set of scribbles and handwritten notes from the course, the word that I saw on every page was *service*. Yoga is about serving others without expectations; it is about balancing your mind and your body for purification; and it is about using your heart to pump out as much unconditional love to the Universe as possible.

The more I thought about the legal information currently out there for yoga professionals, the more I realized that I needed to write this book in order to serve yoga professionals. I have given workshops on Yoga Law all around the world – in India, Kenya, South Korea, Canada and the United States – and the most consistent feedback that I have received from attendees is that the information I provided was helpful. People have told me that because they had learned the *practical* legal aspects of running their business, they felt more confident and capable of turning their dreams into reality. As a lawyer and yoga teacher, I couldn't have asked for anything more.

I feel compelled to write this book for a greater good, without any expectations. If I was interested in making as much money as possible, I assure you that I would not be focusing so much time and energy on Yoga Law. My goal in writing this book is to serve yoga professionals by providing important legal information in a way that is entertaining and fun (yes, FUN!).

Whether you are starting your yoga business, protecting your yoga business, or growing your yoga business, the following pages will explain the basics of what you need to know and get your mind thinking in the right way. If writing this book can change one person's life and business for the better, then it will be entirely worthwhile.

The second reason why I am writing this book is that 99 percent of legal information accessible to the public sucks. Yes, I said it. Law is an integral part of our society and responsible for many of the structures that organize our lives. But most of the system thrives on the fact that a select few have access to a legal education. This elite few charge lots of money for legal services and speak a language that others cannot understand ("legalese"). They traditionally aren't awesome and friendly people who just want to lend a helping hand. Of course, there are countless lawyers who dedicate their lives to offering legal aid, defending people who cannot afford representation and standing up for causes that matter most, like the environment. But unfortunately, these inspirational warriors are the minority of the legal population, drowning in a sea of suits and coffee cups.

The gap in access to legal information is nearly insurmountable. In my experience, the legal profession is anachronistic and archaic, deeply rooted in tradition and with little ambition to change. For the most part, the select few in the elite legal club have a really good thing going, so why would they want to change it? The people who lose in this scenario are the ones who do not have enough money to pay for legal services or a legal education. These are often the people who need help the most.

Now, when I say that the legal information currently available to the public at large sucks, I do not mean that it is inaccurate or unhelpful. The information currently available can be extremely helpful. The problem is that in order to benefit from it, you need to adapt to the legal system. Most of the legal books for entrepreneurs or health and wellness professionals that I have read are complex and intimidating to read. They reference seminal cases, important passages from judgements or complex discussions on fine points of law. Is this helpful? It can be, but only if you have a legal education and spend lots of time reading cases.

What I have learned from running my own law firm is that people are not interested in reading legal cases or precedents; *they just want to know what to do.* They do not care about what a judge said or what case overturned another case; they just need practical information. Think about the students in your yoga classes. For the most part, they are not interested in Patanjali's Yoga Sutras or passages of The Bhagavad Gita that explain the benefits of what you are doing in class. They typically want to do their asanas, get out of class and then check their phone. So, we give them what they want.

By writing this book, I am getting the legal system to *adapt to you and your way of thinking*, instead of the other way around. The information in these pages is prepared for you to easily understand and practically apply. I have not written all of the information that I could possibly share, but I have provided enough to get you informed and keep you awake in the process (I hope). Almost everything you need to know to get started is contained in these pages.

I know you. I have built my businesses for you. I have gone for more than a thousand coffees with people exactly like you. I love you. And, because of this, I am giving you the information you need and giving it to you how you need it. In this book I will share fun and entertaining stories about things that have happened to me or to my clients (with their permission of course, so no worries about confidentiality). I have tried to share these stories with humour and humility. No fancy words and nothing you have not seen before. This is a simple serving of the basics for you to enjoy. It is my intention that you do so.

Each chapter in this book highlights different legal principles and tells stories to illustrate them. I have chosen to focus on the legal issues that I believe you are most likely to encounter on your journey as a yoga professional. Each chapter contains simple checklists and takeaways to remember. This allows you to easily access the relevant legal principles and remember what is important when you deal with them in the future. Too easy, no?

Lastly, my final reason for writing this book is that I want to give back to yoga, a practice that has improved my quality of living and levels of happiness more than anything else. When I moved to Victoria, British Columbia for a semester of law school in May 2012, I visited some of the town's yoga studios at the recommendation of my friend Jesse Goodman, who said that yoga was a big part of the local culture. My first steps on a yoga mat were rooted in tourism and nothing else. I fell in love immediately and was hooked. Initially, I loved the fact that I could be awake and silent for an hour of the day. Something clicked. My body felt better, I was more aware of my breath and I was more peaceful in almost all situations of my life. This was the start of a journey that has changed who I am, how I live my life and how I treat others. Yoga is the most precious gift.

Knowing how yoga changed my life, I am writing this book to help YOU, the amazing yoga professional who is making a difference in the lives of millions of people. You may be teaching at a studio with hundreds of clients, running a teacher training course, organizing a festival or just practicing by yourself. The point is, you are making a difference in the world and I bow to you in gratitude. This book is my offering to help you continue to make a difference in the world with a better understanding of the law. It is a humble and perhaps miniscule contribution to such a vast field, but it feels like the right thing to do. All of the words in this book have been written with a full heart and unconditional love. May you receive their message in such a way.

Chapter 1

The New Legal Paradigm

Intention

I want to start by explaining what Yoga Law is and why we need it now more than ever. I want to empower you by showing you how closely the law intertwines with your business and your dreams; how yoga professionals often make the same simple mistakes; and how you can avoid making those same mistakes. I will also share the "Pay me now or pay me later" principle that reveals the importance of being proactive when operating within the law.

If you remember only one thing from this chapter, remember that you will inevitably interact with the law as you build a business and that it is best to be proactive in doing so, for your professional health, your bank account and your peace of mind.

What Is Yoga Law and Why Do We Need It?

Yoga Law represents a shift in the current legal paradigm. It provides a conscious and heart-leading understanding and use of the law specifically for yoga professionals. But why? Why does it matter if amazing entrepreneurs and yoga community leaders understand how to use the law? This is a fair question that I am confronted with each time I give a Yoga Law lecture at a conference or at a yoga teacher training. I have given presentations all across the world, in all sorts of different venues, and the same question constantly surfaces: Why do we need Yoga Law? Let's answer this question in two parts.

Firstly, the "Yoga" Aspect of Yoga Law: Why do yoga professionals need their own approach to understanding and using the law? This is an easy one. For the most part, yogis are amazing at helping students, building communities and inspiring others to follow a yogic lifestyle. Their gifts are incredible and invaluable. However, to put it frankly, the ability to properly structure and run a business is not one of the strengths that yogis traditionally possess. Yogis often lead with the heart and focus on serving others first, without expectations. They are attuned to spiritual energies and tapped into the Universe; they are holders of sacred histories and ancient practices with powerful mystical qualities.

It may be due to these unique skills and abilities that most yogis feel stressed, anxious or overwhelmed when it comes to handling anything related to their business that they do not already know about. Also, because they are trained chiefly to serve others, yogis can sometimes forget to let themselves and their best interests figure in a business equation. They can live off week-to-week schedules of studio classes and private lessons, forgetting to look up and see the bigger picture. I love my yoga instructors and yogi friends, so my heart breaks when I hear that they are burnt out from teaching too many classes or that their studios have not treated them properly. Yogis give their life to such a special cause and our society in the West does not always reward them justly for doing so.

From the very beginning, I have wanted to help these amazing yoga professionals share their gifts with the world and empower them to live their dream life along the way. When I first began working with yoga clients (which started out as helping friends), I saw the same patterns emerge over and over again. The same stories of yogis feeling comfortable with certain things while totally neglecting others. I gave these clients some business and legal coaching and was shocked at what happened next. *These yogis suddenly grasped important concepts and began building incredible businesses.* Once I had explained basic principles in a comfortable way, they immediately understood and knew how to reach their goals. All I had to do was turn the key to the car and the engine began running itself.

So here is what I have learned while helping my yoga clients: *There is nothing about being a yogi that precludes you from succeeding in business or operating a business professionally.* It is just a matter of approaching legal concepts on terms that you feel comfortable with as a yogi. Most yogis do not understand the law the way that other business professionals do. This is a beautiful thing and is a wonderful opportunity for all of us to learn. It has inspired me to communicate basic legal precepts in ways that yogis will understand – on their terms, in their language. Through the power of storytelling and relatable examples, yogis can understand what they need to understand about the law.

Secondly, the "Law" Aspect of Yoga Law: Why do yoga professional need to understand and use the law? The best answer I can offer is the same one that I give at my lectures: The law can help you. And you, my friend, need all the help you can get. Starting your own business and trying to make a career in the yoga or wellness field has never been more difficult than it is today. The competition is fierce and almost every aspect of the market is saturated. But the industry is booming: more and more people are putting yoga and health at the forefront of their lives, investing in their wellbeing as much as their retirement plans. In this unique marketplace filled with options and opportunities, only the strong will survive.

So where does the law fit into all this? Well, the law pervades every part of our society. If you have decided to participate in society in the West, you will inevitably interact with the law. If you are working for yourself, working for others or performing any sort of service, there are laws that apply to everything you do. I encourage you to accept this. Be empowered by it. Because there has never been so much at stake (more on that in a second).

To explain how the law can help you, I would like to turn to a metaphor that one of my favourite law school professors, John Page, used to describe how the law operates. He explained that the law can *work as a shield and a sword*. This metaphor has always stuck with me. I often use it to explain the strategic approach I take when helping my clients. The law is a shield because it helps you defend and protect your business, but the law is also a sword because it can be used as a tool to grow and conquer. Without the law, you go off to battle without the right equipment and do not stand a chance of survival. Would you do yoga without a mat? Could you perform pranayama without awareness of your breath? That would be like running a business without the law.

Here's the bottom line: *the law should be seen as a tool to grow your business and a tool to protect your business.* The sooner you can grasp this basic premise, the sooner you will change your relationship with the law. There are two different kinds of business owner – the ones who say, "I just don't get contracts," and the others who say, "I love using contracts to communicate openly and honestly with everyone, so they feel valued and we can enjoy amazing relationships." I am taking a stand for you to be the latter kind of business owner. Since I firmly believe in abundance, I also hold faith that everyone who empowers themselves with the basic legal information in this book can accomplish all of their dreams and crush all of their goals.

The Stakes Have Never Been Higher: Your Dream Life Awaits

You will only change your relationship with the law once you realize how much is at stake. Until you have something to lose, you will not really care to change your behaviour. Bob Dylan wrote, "If you've got nothing, you've got nothing to lose." This applies to humans across every field of their life: change only happens when you realize that you care more for what you want than what you currently have.

Let me remind you that the stakes have never been higher. We are talking about your life and dreams here yogis, wake up! You are building a business for yourself, for your family and for your legacy. You get to make your mark on the world. You are going to invest so much time, effort and money into your business that it only makes sense to do it properly and put yourself in the best position to succeed.

I want to draw your attention to a critical distinction between "what is at stake" and the reason "why'" you are running your business. Your "why" may be something like: I want to offer a safe space for women to connect with each other and build love through body image and through yoga asana practice. However, what is at stake in your business is the consequence of you successfully achieving your "why." And what exactly is at stake if you succeed? Only everything! Your ability to impact people, your ability to live your dream life and your ability to be the change you want to see in the world.

What is at stake if you do not succeed? Only everything! You may deprive others of your gift. You may lose the opportunity to touch another person and improve their life. You may have to go back to your office job.

We should *always* keep in mind that we are taking a professional approach to our lives and our businesses because of what is at stake.

I will share a personal example. In May 2017, I decided out of nowhere that I wanted to take my law firm online. This wasn't in the business plan, but no biggie. My Muskoka Yoga Festival co-founder Ashley told me that she had booked a ticket for Bali and would be travelling from early Autumn until April. I wanted to do that, too. I love to travel! So I did. I decided that I would take my business online and travel the world. *This was my dream and I was determined to make it work.* I was always terrified that being a lawyer meant I would have to spend endless hours in an office hating my life. But if I could travel and still be a lawyer, I knew I could do anything. More importantly, I knew that I could show people in other professional fields that they could do anything, too. This is what I really wanted – to prove to myself that I could do anything and inspire the same belief in others. Once you know you can do anything, well… you can do anything!

A few months into my business transformation, I had an incredible realization. My own eureka moment. I was in Agonda, India and my Internet cut out during a video-conference meeting with a dream client. I hopped on my scooter, drove to a nearby café, and scrambled to get online and continue the meeting. Once the meeting resumed, the prospective client told me, "Cory, we appreciate your time, but frankly we have concerns about working with you because of the distance between us and you being abroad." I was livid.

This person was questioning my ability to live my dream. This person was saying, "Sorry Cory, your dream life just won't do. If you want clients, you'll have to come back to Vancouver and sit in an office." It was at this moment that I realized something massive was at stake. If I was unable to get this client and blow their socks off with amazing service, I would have to pack up my bags and go home. The dream I had dreamed would never be a reality. I would not stand for that. *I was determined to succeed because so much was at stake.* I ended up getting the client, doing incredible work for them, adding value to their business and seeing their business thrive.

In this personal example, my reason "why" in running Conscious Counsel – offering heart-leading legal services to amazing people doing incredible things – was very different from what was at stake. What was at stake was my ability to live my dream life of being a lawyer while travelling the world, meeting new people, learning new languages and eating yummy different foods. And, most importantly, showing other people that they can live their dream lives as well.

So, *find out what is at stake in the success of your business.* If you know, write it down right now. Otherwise, go meditate and dream up the most wonderful life possible for you and your business, and then write that down. Any time someone challenges you or says your dream is not possible, just visualize that piece of paper, know that you can do it and then make magic happen. Your determination to live your dreams will be stronger than someone else's objection. If you have the resolve to succeed, nothing can get in your way.

How does understanding what is at stake connect to Yoga Law? Whatever is at stake for you will involve a thriving business that supports you, your family and your community. You will need the law to achieve that thriving business. There is no way around it. Anyone who is thinking about running a successful business will inevitably have to deal with the law (unless the law deals with them first). If I am repeating myself, I am doing it intentionally. In order for you to succeed, it is absolutely necessary that you learn to see the law as both a shield and a sword to protect and grow your business. So, find out what is at stake – your dreams and your goals – and use that as a motivation to embrace the law. Get excited that by writing and signing legal agreements, you are protecting your dreams and bringing them that much closer to reality.

Everyone Makes the Same Mistakes – THEY DO!

If you are not convinced that Yoga Law is necessary, this next sentence is going to floor you. I saved my best reason for last and I firmly believe it is bulletproof. No one can deny its existence or its application to your life. Ready? Sure? Okay, here goes: *Everyone makes the same mistakes with the law.* I have worked with hundreds of clients, met thousands of wellness professionals from all over the world, and they are all doing the same basic things wrong. Almost none of them are writing and signing the right types of agreements, protecting their intellectual property effectively, or stopping opportunities from going to waste by using the law to their advantage.

Do I blame these wonderful people? No way, Jose! I would make the exact same mistakes if I had not gone to law school. But I did go to law school and I have seen different people make the same mistakes over and over again. Worst of all, the mistakes are so easy to fix. If I really believed these problems were too complex to handle, I would not go through all this effort to share the information in this book with you. The good news for all of us is that we can do a few simple things to fix these mistakes. I greatly look forward to sharing this information with you in the following chapters, all of which deal with a relevant legal topic.

Story: "Pay Me Now or Pay Me Later"

I want to close this chapter by sharing a story that really drives home the benefits of being proactive in understanding and using the law. This is a story about a very important lesson that I learned at the beginning of my legal career. It is one of my favourite stories because I have carried the lesson with me through all of my work with yoga professionals ever since.

On my first day officially practicing law, I had lunch with an old mentor from the law firm Dentons. He was a partner at the firm and had built a very strong legal practice for himself. During my time as an articling student at Dentons, we had bonded and become friends. Now he was graciously and generously inviting me to lunch at a fancy restaurant in downtown Vancouver. I assumed that in addition to congratulating me, he would give an inspiring and compelling pep talk about being a lawyer who could finally contribute to the legal system.

We greeted each other with a hug. "Congratulations," he said wholeheartedly, looking me in the eyes. "Now that you are a lawyer," he said sternly, "I am going to give you the most important piece of advice that I can share." He was staring into my soul. I could feel it. "Being a lawyer is very different from being a law student. You are now representing clients and their problems become your problems. They are hiring you to use your expertise in their best interest. Always take that privilege seriously." I was etching his words into stone in my mind so that I would never forget them. He wasn't done yet.

"Listen up, because this is the most important piece of

advice that you must share with your clients." The moment was here. I was nearly salivating; I had waited years to hear this. Three years of law school and one year of articling. He paused dramatically to ensure that he had my attention, and then finally continued: "When you meet with your clients, they may not want to pay for your services. They will think that they can do things on their own and that downloading contracts from the Internet will suffice. But you are going to tell them with an open and honest heart: You can pay me now or you can pay me later." He looked at me to make sure I got the point. He then repeated this sage advice. "You are going to tell your clients that they can pay you now or they can pay you later. And you will tell them to pay you now because it will be significantly cheaper and will save them sleepless months, if not years."

My mentor went on to explain the reasons for this advice. He told me that 90 percent of my clients would do everything they could to keep their expenses as low as possible at the start. (This made sense to me because I thought the same way whenever I paid for professional services: "How can I get as much as possible while paying as little as possible?" Value.) He said that my clients would convince themselves they could copy contracts from friends or draft them on their own, finding every excuse to cut corners when it comes to the law. But he stressed that any client who is serious about growing a healthy business will at some point need a lawyer or a basic understanding of how their business interacts with the law. They can only achieve so much before running into problems. If they start with a proper understanding of the law, they will be able to use legal agreements to actually build their business. So, he continued: "Tell your clients that they will have to deal with you at some point, so they might as well do it for a cheaper price before the problems begin. They can pay you now or they can pay you later. Your encouragement, their choice."

Following these words, we did not return to the subject of the law or lawyering. My mentor had shared with me what he deemed most important about being a lawyer and believed that he had equipped me with the necessary tools to build a strong legal practice. We then began an activity that I have perfected over the past thirty-three years of my life: talking about sports.

My mentor's advice was not what I had expected to hear, but it later proved to be immensely helpful to my clients. After I had spent some months working with clients, I began to understand why this advice was the sole piece of wisdom that my mentor had shared with me. At first I thought all of my clients' problems were unique, but after a while certain patterns became clear. Over and over again I saw my clients frustrated and scared by issues stemming from the exact same sources: not understanding their contracts, or not knowing what provisions they needed to have in their contracts, or not having any contracts in place at all.

By the time I noticed the patterns in my clients' legal issues, I had developed a cool and calm demeanour about finding the solutions. I knew that everything was going to be okay (this mantra has never failed me) and that I would find a way to solve the problem. Clearly, I could not help clients who had already made mistakes in the past, except by doing all I could to help get them out of trouble. But this did not keep me from holding out hope that I could help new clients who were just starting out. As my practice grew and I spent more and more hours lawyering, I saw the truth in my mentor's advice and how simple it was to help clients avoid making mistakes from the beginning. My clients just had to be open and proactive in using the law.

I soon started to wonder: If people are willing to spend so much money on frivolous things in their life, like avocados for example (that is a joke, I love avocados), why would they not spend money on legal documents? There had to be more than meets the eye, so I began to dig a bit deeper. Could lawyers be the problem...?

Your Chapter Checklist

This is what I hope you've taken away from this chapter:

- The law is a tool that can help you build your business.
- Once you know what goals and dreams are at stake in the success of your business, you will be open to using better legal practices to achieve business success.
- Lawyers are your friends and care about seeing you live your dream life.
- Everyone makes the same basic mistakes around the law. Those mistakes are super easy to fix if you are open and proactive in dealing with the law.

Chapter 2

Why Everyone Hates Lawyers but Really Shouldn't

Intention

I am now going to tackle the most notorious stereotypes that surround lawyers, show you why they are not true and invite you to change your relationship with the law. Just like in vipassana, where the first three days of meditation clear the mind of distractions so that the technique can be properly taught, we must first clear our minds of everything we think we know about the law and lawyers so that we can receive new information properly. Once we reach that point, I will do my best to change the way you look at the law and how it governs your life.

If you remember only one thing from this chapter, remember that the law governs the many different relationships you have in your life and your business. By understanding and using the law, you are trying to find a way to communicate your expectations in these relationships openly, clearly and honestly.

Why Everyone Hates Lawyers

If you could have asked me one question when you found out I was a lawyer, what would you have asked? I am constantly baffled when I speak at professional events because the same question always follows me around: "Do you watch *Suits*?" To add insult to injury, it seems that everyone who asks me this question thinks that they are the first person to ask it. They will take a small step back with a smile already on their face. I can tell they are thinking to themselves: I knew it, I knew it, he watches *Suits*! I have spent thousands of hours studying at law school, working in big law and running my own law firm. I have so much knowledge to share about the law and yet people always ask me about a television show. So just in case you are curious, I am going to answer the question right now: I have done everything I can to live a life without suits and I avoid them in every aspect, television included. No suits for me!

Luckily I learned not to take things personally very early in my adult life (especially after reading the wonderful book *The Four Agreements* by Don Miguel Ruiz), so I have never thought that the whole *Suits* thing was about me. Instead, I have constantly thought about why I am asked this question. Why do people care if I watch a television show about lawyers? One day it hit me. People think that being a lawyer in real life is like being a lawyer in Suits. They think that a television show portrays reality. Law firms are filled with beautiful people wearing, *ahem...* suits, who get the key piece of evidence at the last second to break the case. All lawyers make the wittiest rebuttals on demand and most of them have a drinking problem. Only one of these stereotypes *might* be true in real life and I will leave the guessing to your imagination.

As with many other aspects of life, television and film have totally skewed public perception by misrepresenting the legal system and lawyers. Fortunately, most of the population never has to go to court and never travels further than the ostentatious meeting rooms of a law firm. But this means that they have no idea what actually goes on in the day-to-day life of a lawyer.

They have no idea about the law. Regardless of whether they believe they "can't handle the truth," they are out of touch with what the law and the legal system are really about.

On top of this, lawyers in real life don't have an excellent reputation. They are typically thought to be ruthless, heartless and very wealthy. Such character attributes probably stem from Hollywood, but they can find validation in day-to-day encounters. People love telling me about other lawyers they have met in their lives. It is like they have been waiting all day to randomly meet a lawyer to complain and yell about their experience. Sometimes their eyes become bloodshot with rage as if smoke is about to emerge from their ears. They usually tell me how high their legal fees were and how rude opposing counsel was to them. These conversations seem to be a healing process for them, so I usually just stand there and take it. Eventually I will politely say, "I get it. I do. You don't like lawyers. But please consider that I'm just standing in line to buy a coffee like you. At least let me have my first sip before you continue."

On a personal level, outside of my professional life, I think the public perception of lawyers has hurt me more than it has helped me, specifically when it comes to dating. The amount of times that I have been rejected after sharing my vocation is slightly staggering. "I dated a lawyer once and all he cared about was his work" is a classic one. I also get the occasional "My last boyfriend was a lawyer. He was such a jerk," to which I never really know what to say. If I ever hear, "I was once married to a lawyer…" I will know that it's time to run. I do not need to hear the end of that sentence.

Funnily enough, I too have misconstrued what it really means to be a lawyer. Yes, even a lawyer can be confused about what being a lawyer is like. It was October 2015 and

I had recently been hired as an associate at Altman and Co., a Vancouver-based business and entertainment law firm. My first job as a lawyer after being called to the bar! That year the firm was an official sponsor of the Whistler Film Festival. Before I started work at the firm, I was invited to join the other lawyers in Whistler for the weekend activities. What a blast! I got dressed up and carried lots of business cards that read: *Entertainment Lawyer.* There were dinners and film screenings and parties and networking events. I was born for this. *I loved being an entertainment lawyer.* Then on Monday I came into the office and was handed a bunch of entertainment law files that needed to be completed on tight deadlines. Soon afterwards, I was fighting to keep my eyes open. Endless piles of paper replaced flashy smiles and cheeky small talk. I quickly learned that my time in Whistler was the *rare exception.* The general rule for life as an entertainment lawyer was long hours of paperwork hunched over a computer. *I hated being an entertainment lawyer.* Busted. I had let my imagination of a lawyer's life whisk me away to dreams far from reality.

While I can't and won't speak to the veracity of the exciting and sometimes insulting stereotypes that surround lawyers, I will say this: *Most of what you think you know about lawyers is totally wrong.* I know this because I'm a lawyer. I've worked in a whole bunch of different legal environments with a whole bunch of different lawyers, and I haven't really seen anything exciting. It's not an exciting job. I've been lucky enough to do lots of exciting things in my life and being a lawyer is not really one of them. Yes, helping amazing people achieve their dreams is inspiring and purpose-filled, but drafting legal documents is not. There are some thrilling moments for sure, but generally speaking lawyers spend a lot of time late at night, early in the morning, and all throughout the day sitting at a computer, reading, writing and dissecting documents. The curtain has been pulled and the wizard revealed. We're not in Kansas anymore.

All of this is important because one day I deduced something very interesting. I was sitting in the sauna at Equinox's West Georgia club and having the same conversation I always have when I tell someone that I'm a lawyer. I couldn't help but wonder the following: If people can think they know so much about lawyers and still be wrong in their pre-conceived notions, what do they think about the law? They probably think that the law is an inaccessible and insurmountable mountain of information they will never understand. If they think lawyers have to be a certain way in order to practice law, and if they do everything they can to distance themselves from lawyers, naturally they will distance themselves from the law too. The more I tested this hypothesis, the more I came to believe it was true. I would ask friends and strangers questions like: Who is your lawyer? What do you know about the law? Time and time again they replied that they didn't like lawyers, didn't trust lawyers, didn't have enough money for lawyers or felt too intimidated by the law to even start working with a lawyer. People actually made an effort to stay away from the law and lawyers because they felt so uncomfortable. *This was worse than I thought.*

I learned all that I needed to know during a conversation in Hawaii while attending the Wanderlust Yoga Festival with a stranger who eventually became a friend and client. I was waiting in line to pay at a coffee shop and offered the person beside me some pomegranate seeds. She accepted and we got to talking. When I told her that I was a lawyer, she said, "No way, you are too nice to be a lawyer." She told me about her booming business that was growing at warp speed, so I asked, "Who is your lawyer? What do your distribution agreements look like?" She just looked at her feet. The silence said everything. She went on to tell me why she did not like lawyers, how expensive they were and why she did not want to work with them. Alarmed, I responded: "But your business is at risk," I said shocked. This was way worse than I thought. "We're going to fix this," I said confidently and then bit down on a bunch of pomegranate seeds, causing the pomegranate juice to spray all over her white shirt, covering it in deep red colouring. I looked at her sheepishly and we both broke out in laughter. "And, I'm going to fix your shirt too," I said with equal passion and conviction.

Shoshin: A Beginner's Mind

All of the discomfort people feel regarding the law means that I have a problem on my hands whenever I prepare for a public Yoga Law talk. I have so much information that can help so many people, but a lot of attendees will close themselves off from hearing it because it is coming from a lawyer and has to do with the law. So at the beginning of my talks I often ask people to apply the Zen Buddhist concept of shoshin when they think about lawyers and the law.

Shoshin is a concept that invites a master to approach activities or situations they have encountered thousands of times through the eyes of a beginner. The idea is that even though we are doing something we have done many times before, we will look at it with the fresh eyes of someone who is doing it for the first time, and thereby allow ourselves to appreciate it for *what it really is*, not what we think it is.

This outlook can be applied to anything in your life – the way you look at your partner, the way you feel about your dog, the amazing feeling you have after a sip of coffee or tea. Imagine if every time you looked at your child, parent or partner, you saw them as if you were seeing them for the first time. Would you love them differently? Would you care that they did not clean up their room or left the toilet seat up? No! You would give them a massive kiss because you know they are what matters most in your life. Shoshin… if only we could always maintain this perspective.

At my Yoga Law talks, I invite everyone in the audience to drop all the stories they have heard about the law and lawyers, and *then imagine what I am about to tell them is the first thing they have ever heard about lawyers or the law.* Once I get everyone's assurance that they are committed to seeing with new and fresh eyes, I go into the crowd, take someone's hand, look deeply into their eyes and say, "Lawyers are your friends and the law is a tool to help you grow your business." Laughter. Every time. There has never been a time that the crowd has not broken out in laughter. I do play it up a little – the dramatic pause, holding tension in the room – but only to make a point that is worth making *because it is true.*

After the laughter subsides, I really bring home my point. I ask everyone to close their eyes and listen to my voice, and then I speak very slowly in a deep tone: "This is the first time you've ever heard anything about the law or lawyers. You never knew these things existed before." Then I repeat myself at a glacial pace: "Lawyers are your friends who care about you and want to see you live your dreams. The law is a tool you use to help you grow your business." The second time always works better. I ask the group to open their eyes and notice that suddenly their laughter has been replaced with head nods and a belief that such an outlook is possible. Just as Daniel-San needed to "wax on" and "wax off" without knowing why as he learned karate, I need people to clear their minds in order to make space for a new way of learning about the law.

So now I extend this opportunity to you. I can assure you

that as long as you hold on to your limiting beliefs about the law, you will deprive yourself of the benefits of this book. You will continue to have a blocked relationship with the law that will hurt you more than it will help you. I am here to help. Take the next two minutes and think about all the juicy and fantastic stories you have heard about lawyers and the legal system – bathe in them, revel in them (isn't this fun?!). Now, once your two minutes are up, you need to do something a little bit scary: you need to drop these stories. All of them are choices you have made about how to see a particular thing. They are interpretations you have turned into truths. Next, close your eyes and imagine that you do not know anything about the law. You have never heard about it. What I am going to say next is the first thing you have ever heard about the law.

Lawyers are your friends and the law is a tool to help you grow your business. Believe it. Breathe it. Embrace this new reality. Okay. We're ready.

Relationships

Now that we are looking at the law in a brand new way, I am going to make it very easy for you to understand how the law works. The law is really a bunch of rules around the different relationships you have in your life. Through centuries of governments and parliaments and rules, we have ended up with systems that apply laws to almost everything we do on a daily basis. I could break this down to a miniscule level, but that would be boring – and I promised you that this would be simple and fun. So, all you need to know is that the law dictates how we should behave in almost every situation of our lives.

So, the law is everywhere. Got it. Now that you understand

the law's pervasiveness and relevance to our lives, it is only sensible to embrace it instead of skirting it.

Next I want you to think about all the different categories of relationships in your life. For the moment, let's keep it personal. You have your family, your friends, your pet (obviously the best), your co-workers – and the list goes on and on. Even within these general categories, there are sub-categories. For family, you have your immediate family, your cousins, your spouse's family and so on. For friends, you have friends from your hometown, friends from high school, friends from university, friends you played sports with, *ad infinitum*. After you have done this for a bit, just stop and take a quick rest. The point of thinking about all of the people in your life as falling into a category is to direct your mind to thinking about relationships in a different way, which will be helpful in the Relationships Exercise that follows.

I hope it has been cool for you to reflect on all of the amazing people in your life. These are the lives you have touched with your love and the people who have made you who you are. I am sure that you have thought about some EPIC people you love to the moon, who have totally made your life the amazing journey that it is. Perfect. Stick with these people. There were probably some names or faces that came up and made you think: "Oh god – not that person, I cannot stand that person." Noticing that some people do not make you the best version of yourself is really important, so good job.

I will state the obvious by reminding you that life is too short not to be surrounded by incredible people who raise your vibrations. Environment is everything. If someone isn't making you better, they are making you worse. And when there is so much at stake in your life, we need you at your best. So, find a way to minimize relations with such people or cut them out entirely. If you need an excuse, tell them a lawyer told you that you had to. "Sorry, it was great being friends, but a lawyer told me that I can only hang out with people who totally stoke my fire of awesomeness."

The Relationships Exercise

I want you to turn to a fresh page in your journal (all yogis have journals, right?) or grab a piece of scrap paper and do the following:

1. At the top of the page write *My Professional Relationships* and underline it. If you love using colours to make your writing look pretty, this is your moment to do so.

2. In the middle of the page, write the word *Me* and circle it. Are we both staring at the same page with the word *Me* circled in the middle? Great.

3. Just as you broke down your personal relationships into categories, now think about all of your professional relationships in the different areas of your work and separate them into categories. Write these categories on your page and draw a line connecting each one to the word Me.

4. Next, under each category, try your best to write down everyone you work with in that category and then draw a line connecting them back to the category. Here are examples of how your page might start to look:

    I. If you are a yoga teacher, you may have drawn lines connecting the word Me to categories like "Yoga Studios Where I Teach," "My Students," "My Retreat" and "Private Students." Under "Yoga Studios," you may want to list the different studios where you teach and the manager at each one.

Under "My Retreat," you may want to create sub-categories like "Clients," "Venue," "Co-Teachers" – and then keep going until you have clarified the relationships in each sub-category.

II. If you own a yoga studio, you may have drawn lines connecting the word Me to categories like "My Landlord," "My Staff," "Studio Members," "Online Customers," "My Bookkeeper/Lawyer," and "Mindbody Online." Under "My Staff," you may want to list sub-categories like "Employees," "Yoga Teachers at the Studio" and "Studio Volunteers." Try to break down each group with as much specificity as possible.

III. If you run a yoga teacher training, you may have drawn lines connecting the word *Me* to categories like "Faculty," "Students," "Venue." Try to keep going and break all of these categories into sub-categories until you have laid out all of your relationships.

5. Take a well-deserved break. We don't need to complete this exercise in one sitting and it would be better to keep working on it whenever you get some more time to think about it. When I did the exercise myself, I found that I kept coming back to my page and remembering new and different relationships that I have developed in my business. Leave your page somewhere you can see it and meditate on the topic for a few days.

6. Once you have done as good a job as you can in this exercise, take a good look at your piece of paper. Put it up on the fridge or the wall and stare at it from a distance. These are all of the people with whom you have working relationships. This is important because

now we can start to understand what is required to keep up these different relationships: *All of the relationships require some form of mutual agreement as to what each person will get from and give to the relationship.*

Why Relationships Matter

I would like to reiterate the importance of having good relationships in business. Your relationships, your reputation and how you treat people are the most important aspects of your business – and of your life. If I could share only one key to succeeding in business (and in life), I would say, "Treat people with love." Treat them kindly, put their concerns before yours, and do not always think, "What can I get out of this?" but instead, "How can I best serve this person and give them what they want?" Truly *magical* things happen when you put others before yourself. Be friends with everyone you work with because being friends is easy, fun and free. All of this comes with the precondition that you are working with people you like and want to do great work for. (Remember that whole exercise of cutting out relationships that don't serve you? Here is why it matters.)

Few business relationships are perfect, but if you make friends everything becomes easier. In this context, friendship does not mean that you hang out on the weekends or go to museums together or take weekend trips to Portland. It just means that you have a general interest in that person's life and in seeing them happy. The friendship might only go so far as a coffee date that mixes personal and professional – but it is still a friendship. When you show a person that you genuinely care about them (instead of just caring about yourself, which is something our entire species has mastered), that person will care about you too. And when people care about each other the world becomes a better place. And, when you care about the people you work with, you will be even more motivated to do a great job and ensure that they are satisfied with your services. They will feel the same way for you. Everyone wins!

How does the law fit into all of this? Good relationships are a very important tool in avoiding legal conflicts, should they arise. In 99 percent of cases, when you have a disagreement with a person you have always treated with love and respect, they will work with you to resolve the issue. I can tell you this because I have seen it over and over again when working with clients. All of the disputes that I have helped my clients negotiate have stemmed from an unhealthy relationship. It has never been the case that two people who were friends ended up suing each other. For this reason, I am very selective about my clients and will turn down work if I do not feel an energetic connection with the person I am helping. I have learned from the early stages of building my business that a few thousand dollars is never worth the headache of working with someone you do not like or get along with. Please, always remember this.

The first thing that I tell my clients is to invest in your relationships above everything else. Before I draft any legal agreements or provide any legal advice, I will explain that the best thing they can do for their business is to ensure that their working relationships are healthy relationships. If you do not like someone, stop working with them. Commit to this because it is the most important thing you can do to save yourself from problems in the future. And if you love working with someone, *ask the Universe to send you more people like that to work with*. This is the most valuable and practical business advice I can ever give you. The more you invest in your relationships, the less likely it becomes that you will ever need legal services.

I have always believed in the power of creating healthy relationships with clients in my work as a lawyer. I do not always fit in with my fellow lawyers in that respect. I have noticed that some lawyers have a powerful sense of fear about the prospect of a disgruntled client. This may be because clients who are dissatisfied with a lawyer's services can formally lodge a complaint with the Law Society. They can even try to sue if the lawyer has acted negligently in serving their best interests. When I worked at other law firms, I heard co-workers say things like, "We have to protect ourselves to make sure the client doesn't sue us." I always sat there and scratched my head because I did not understand this fear-based thinking. On one occasion I responded, "What if we also have a great relationship with our client, so that if something goes wrong we can work with them to resolve the issue?" This comment was met with cold stares and angry eyes – and I quickly learned not to bring it up again.

Here is a story that illustrates my point about the power of healthy working relationships. Some time ago, I was drafting an agreement for a client that involved a ton of edits and constant back-and-forth between us and the other side. It just so happened that I made a mistake in the final copy of the agreement by dating a provision for the "32nd of May." (I clearly haven't forgotten this error and it still weighs heavily on my mind.) It was not the end of the world because the date was written properly at other places in the agreement – but it was still a mistake. I had a moment of fear before I remembered that I had become friends with my client and had worked tirelessly to complete the work for him on a tight deadline. When I brought up the error, he just said, "Yeah no worries. I figured that was just a simple mistake." And that was it.

When I think about this story now, I cannot help but

wonder how different the outcome might have been if my relationship with the client was different. Luckily, my client and I cared about each another and had always been genuine in our relationship. I am confident that this is the reason why there was no drama and why my blunder never became an issue for the client. I learned two important lessons from this experience: Firstly, never make a drafting error again, no matter how many edits are going back and forth; and secondly, *always have a great relationship with clients, so that if a problem arises we can work together to resolve it.* I have lived by these lessons ever since, and I am committed to always doing so.

To summarize my entire outlook on business relationships in one sentence: *Only work with awesome people and always put their needs before yours.* If you do this, you will put yourself in a wonderful position to succeed and love everything that you do.

Communicating Expectations

This is the juicy part where we can finally put together everything we have learned and see how simple it is to use the law. Just as I have told you to think about the law and lawyers in a new way, I also want you to think about contracts in a new way. In fact, we are going to think about contracts in such a radically new way that we are no longer going to use the "C" word. Instead, we are going to call them *AGREEMENTS*. Doesn't that feel better? *Agreements* is such a better word for these documents because, really, all they do is outline how people agree to behave while doing business together. They are a simple way for people to communicate their expectations for how they will behave when working together. If you think about agreements in this way, you will immediately realize their incredible value and benefit to your sanity and your business.

Communicating expectations is the foundation of all successful relationships, including the working relationships that you mapped out earlier in this chapter. When I use the term *communicating expectations*, what I really mean is "saying what you think should happen in a variety of outcomes of the working relationship." For example, a studio may expect you to show up at the studio fifteen minutes before class starts and then stay fifteen minutes after class to work the desk. Your studio manager may expect you not to miss more than 15 percent of your scheduled classes every month. You may expect your private clients to provide forty-eight hours' notice before cancelling classes. Agreements are really just a way to confirm and memorialize these expectations.

Now, here is the critical part about communicating expectations that everyone screws up. Everyone. Remember I said that there are a few simple mistakes that everyone makes? Well, here is one of them: *Communicating expectations only works if you are radically honest about what your expectations are.* This is such a simple concept but is executed so poorly in reality, usually because people are afraid to say how they really feel. In almost every working relationship there will be something that people aren't super comfortable with, but in an effort to get on with their business or please the other side, they will agree to it anyways. This is a fail. A big, massive fail.

There is something important to note about uncomfortable conversations – they are uncomfortable for a good reason! The conversation is uncomfortable because there is something that does not feel right, something niggling at you just below the surface. There is incredible merit in having this difficult conversation because it is where your opportunity for growth lies. People avoid discomfort, conflict and confrontation at all expenses, but this does not help anyone. All it does is postpone dealing with the problem until months or years down the line, by which time lots of money, time and energy have been spent, making the problem even more difficult and expensive to resolve.

Do you run away from fear or do you run towards it? There is a great quote in Paramahansa Yogananda's *Autobiography* of a Yogi, where Yogananda's guru Sri Yukteshwar speaks about three important lessons he learned as a child. One of the lessons is about challenging fear. His mother had told him that if he looked under his bed when it was dark in his room, there might be a monster under the bed. Immediately upon hearing this, he ran to look under his bed, confronting the fear directly. "Look fear in the face and it will cease to trouble you" was his brilliant, sage advice. *This is how you should approach difficult conversations in your working relationships.*

If there is something that you do not feel right about in your working relationships, you need to acknowledge that and bring it up right away. The longer you let it linger, the less likely you are to address it. This becomes even more difficult once you have started a working relationship. If you used an agreement to communicate your expectations, and if that agreement did not fully and clearly express your expectations, the relationship will fail. So, I will ask you to save everyone time and just say how you feel when you feel it.

There are nuances in the law for each different type of relationship you have. For example, a yoga studio will have different legal obligations and responsibilities to its clients than it will have to its teachers. Partners in a business will have different obligations to each other than they will have to their employees. Throughout this book, we will look at the different types of relationships we have in our businesses and understand the basic legal obligations that exist on each level.

But what matters now is that you truly grasp the concept that law is really just agreements that communicate expectations. The clearer you can be in communicating what you expect from others and what they can expect from you, the easier it will be to have successful working relationships. The better your working relationships, the better your business. The better your business, the more likely you are to materialize what is at stake for your profession and your life. This final outcome is what I want most for you.

We now understand that your business involves different relationships and that you have to communicate your expectations in these relationships clearly. How is any of this new in our understanding of the law? It isn't! This is what the law has always been – different relationships, different responsibilities and agreements to do different things. You have just never thought about it this way before. And, you never really cared to think about it this way before.

Lawyers will look at and evaluate your agreements in a different way than you will. There are a ton of technical rules and relevant provisions that we need to include in your agreements. *But that does not concern you. And it never will. It is not your job; it is your lawyer's job.* You tell your lawyer what you need and they will prepare it for you. This works in the same way that you prepare classes for your students. If one of your students has a back problem, you will arrange the appropriate asana sequence with their condition in mind. The client is not going to learn why you put bharadvajasana before dhanurasana – and frankly, they don't care. You know what they need and you give it to them. Their job is to simply execute it. The same is true of working with a lawyer. Your only job is to determine what relationships exist and figure out what you want from them, and then your lawyer will take care of the rest.

Through this process, you will learn to love the law. You will love the law because you will use it as a means to improve all of your relationships. You finally have an excuse to clarify what you are really looking to build with all of the people you work with. This will be an extremely refreshing and helpful process in evaluating your life and your business – how you tell people what you want and what you can give them. This is not about falling asleep at the table reading long documents that you do not understand. This is about clear communication. Simple English. The outcomes you have always wanted. Damn this is fun!

Your Chapter Checklist

Grasp this and we're golden:
- People generally dislike lawyers because of stereotypes that are inaccurate.
- The law is really just a set of rules for the different relationships you have in your life.
- To have the best relationships, we should practice open and honest communication.
- Agreements are a simple way for people to communicate their expectations for how they will work together.

Chapter 3

Why It's a Bad Idea to Download Contracts from the Internet

Intention

In this chapter we will learn why it is important for you to use an agreement that you understand and that fits your business, instead of using something you do not understand – or even worse, using nothing at all. In the previous chapter I promised that I would not use the "C" word (contract... *shhhh*!), but I will use it here to remind you that *agreement* is a different word for *contract*. I like agreement better because it sounds so much more collaborative and speaks to the intention of the document.

If you remember only one thing from this chapter, remember that you must always understand what you are agreeing to when you work with someone else. Do not sign something if you do not know what it means, because you are agreeing to be legally bound to it – and that could come back to bite you in the butt.

Why Yogis Need Agreements

As a lawyer, I find it funny that working with my yogi clients is so different than working with business professionals from other fields. It is like there is *working with yogis* and then there is working with everyone else. In the yogi realm, business meetings are usually held before or after a yoga class and tea is almost always involved. Strong connections are usually formed and it is always easy to get lost in dreamy conversations about our philosophies, the daily experience of being alive or the infinite power of the Universe. Even as I write this, I think about how cool it is to offer legal services to yogis. Yummy.

Yogis have the compassionate and heart-leading pieces down pat, but when it comes to professionalization, there are tons of opportunities for continued growth. Most yogis I have worked with repeat the same patterns of professional behaviour over and over again (although I must admit that many are equally or even more professional than me!). For some reason, most yogis apparently believe that it is acceptable not to sign written agreements or other types of documents. They assume that because everyone loves each other, things will just always work out. "The Universe will totally take care of that," a client once told me. While I am the Universe's #1 biggest fan, *I know that we also need to help the Universe take care of things.*

The most basic and easiest way that we, as yogis, can slowly professionalize our industry is through the practice of having written agreements. It makes everything simpler and easier. It also shows the world at large that we should be taken seriously – like, "Hey, I'm not just an acai-bowl-eating, ujjayi-breathing, hand-standing yogi. I'm all that and a professional." Everyone benefits when agreements are formed around working relationships. Our clients benefit, our partners benefit, our industry benefits – and we benefit.

What Is an Agreement?

The word agreement pretty much captures the essence of what

is going on: Two or more people are about to work together in some capacity and therefore "agree" to work together on the terms that are outlined in a document. Simply put, agreements are documents that bind parties into performing certain obligations. Write this down. It will make everything so much easier.

A lot of clients will tell me, "I have never used an agreement before," but I quickly point out that they use agreements every day of their life. Using Uber is an agreement. If you have ever had a client or paid someone to do something for you, there is an agreement behind that. Your decision to purchase or download this book is rooted in an agreement. We make agreements with our kids, spouses and friends every day. The difference here is that we are writing out the agreements and specifically outlining what we expect from the relationship. "Oh, that's an agreement!" my clients say once I have pointed out the obvious. With Yoga Law, we are doing all the things we were doing before, just with a bit more clarity and a better understanding of why we are doing them.

Agreements form the backbone of commercial relationships. It is that magical moment when pen hits paper (or when mouse clicks "e-sign here") and the parties finish negotiating a deal that they both feel is a win. Signing an agreement symbolically and practically represents that both parties are agreeing to follow the rules of the game they just agreed to play. When agreements are properly formed and parties agree to their terms, the document becomes *binding*. This means that whoever signs the document will have an obligation to fulfill the duties they agreed to in that document.

Agreements are not just documents – *they are extensions of the respect that the parties have in working with each other*. An agreement is a piece of paper that says, "Because I love you and because I want to have the best relationship possible with you, I'm going to let you know what I can give you when we work together and what I expect from you in return." Written agreements are extremely helpful for your working relationships, because they provide a very easy tool and reference point to see if the parties are doing what they said they would do at the start of the relationship.

For example, let's say you have all of the teachers at your yoga studio sign an agreement with you. In each agreement, as part of the services they will provide, the teachers promise to be at the welcome desk fifteen minutes before and fifteen minutes after class. If a situation arises where a teacher continually fails to do this, you can easily and politely say, "When we invited you to teach in our community, you agreed to do this," and then show them the agreement they signed. At this point, you will be able to communicate with the teacher from a place of clarity and not confrontation. Best of all, you can deal with the situation maturely and respectfully. You are being a real person by saying, "Hey, you agreed to do this and it isn't happening. How can we help?" By no means do you want to whip out the agreement every time a tiny mistake is made, but the clearer you can be in showing people what you agreed to, the easier it can be to fix the problems.

A lot of my clients have assured me that they use verbal agreements. Verbal agreements are great and totally enforceable at law, but I would not describe them as "best practices." This is because two people can understand the same verbal agreement differently. If you only reach a verbal agreement with someone, both of your perspectives on what was agreed will shift and change once your relationship changes. You may begin the relationship on the right foot and love working together at the start, but you will inevitably encounter some challenges as the relationship develops. There may be confusion, finger pointing and allegations about what was or was not agreed to. A written instrument (like emails or text messages) will always help support your understanding of any alleged verbal agreements, so be sure to put as much in writing as possible.

I took a class in law school called Trial Advocacy that was super fun because we learned what it would be like to run our own case in front of a judge. On the first day of lectures, our professor told us, *"It doesn't matter what happens; it matters what you can prove."* Verbal agreements are fine, but they are not the best form of evidence to prove that an agreement was made under definitive terms. The worst-case scenario is a "he said/she said" type of argument. There is nothing inherently wrong about this, but it simply is not the best evidence you can have to support your position. Properly executed agreements are sweet. We want you to be set up to succeed, so do your best to capture your agreements in this way.

Why Downloading Agreements from the Internet Won't Work

Firstly, I want you to know that I totally understand why you would download an agreement from the Internet. I used to download music from Napster and watch full live concerts on YouTube (especially The War on Drugs shows). As human beings in a society where everything is driven by money, we try to cut corners wherever we can. I get it, I really do. I am not discouraging you from downloading contracts or borrowing your friend's contracts for moral or judgmental purposes. I am only doing so for the following reason:

The most common mistakes and problems that I have to fix as a lawyer arise from clients using agreements that are not their own or that they do not fully understand. It is that plain and simple.

I am writing this chapter because I am trying to fix the most consistent problem that I see. People download an agreement they do not understand, steal one from another company or borrow one from a friend, and then they get in trouble when it does not serve their needs or fit their business. At that point, they will have to pay a lawyer to help them get out of the jam, investing at least twice as much as they would have spent if they had drafted the contracts properly in the first place. I will continually repeat the "Pay me now or pay me later" lesson in this book, only because it is so powerfully true.

Unless you fully understand everything that is written in an agreement you have downloaded from the Internet (which is unlikely because it will probably be written in super legal terms), it would be a bad idea to sign it. Even if you do understand everything in the agreement, it would be best to make sure that the terms serve you and your business.

"That Yoga Student"

A tricky part of writing an agreement is knowing what terms to include. This is why "borrowing" a contract from your friend or the Internet does not really help you. That specific contract was designed for your friend's business, which has its own unique set of goals, exposure to risks and other challenges. I totally understand that you may not fully appreciate the repercussions of downloading, stealing or borrowing a contract, so I am going to try to illustrate my point by speaking about "*that* yoga student."

Close your eyes (how can you read with your eyes closed? Ha – got you!) and picture a very particular type of yoga student. We have all met this type of student before. It may be a personal friend, a client or someone you know from your studio. This is the student who does not really get what the whole yoga thing is about but has the best intentions in practicing yoga. The key is to remember that this student subjectively believes that what they are doing is yoga. You cannot fault them for doing what they are doing, but as a yoga teacher you can see how easy it would be to help them deepen and expand their practice for greater growth, if only you could guide them.

Now imagine, this student arrives late to your class. You have a strict rule in your Tuesday 17:30 Vinyasa Flow class that no one is allowed to enter once you have begun meditation, but this student still finds a way to sneak into the back and lie down on their mat. You let them in because you understand that they tried their best to rush to class from the office. As you get into your asana sequence, you notice that this student is using modifications that do not suit their body or their needs. If anything, they are putting themselves at serious risk by trying poses so far outside of their body's ability. They are constantly checking out the students in the front row and trying to copy them. You offer the student an adjustment and ask, "Where did you learn to do vakasana and why are you doing it that way?" They look at you innocently and say, *"This is how I saw my friend do it, so I just tried doing it the same way."*

Next, you move to the sitting asanas and see the student take out a whole bunch of props. They are clearly using the props in the wrong way, putting themselves at risk of injury by using blocks and straps incorrectly. Again, you have to correct them and ask, "Why are you using these props in these poses?" The student does not even have to blink. "Oh, I saw someone who was really good at yoga doing this once, so now I'm doing it just like them." You promptly correct the student once again. Later, you see the same student slowly creeping out of class as you put the group into savasana to rest. They do not even stick around until the end. They are too busy to make time for corpse pose, thus depriving themselves of much needed rest for their body. You know they will not get the benefits of the pose, but there is not much you can do to help them.

Does any of this resonate? I am sure that you have met at least one person who is that student. But remember – *their errors are magnified to you because you know what is right and because you teach or practice yoga all the time.* You know they cannot compare their body to anyone else's, that they need to come prepared to class and that they should only be doing modifications or using props where necessary. In yoga you cannot just do what everyone else is doing because it is an individual exercise, albeit one that takes place in a group setting. Your body will never be like anyone else's and so your practice needs to be customized for you.

Turning back to the law and agreements, the parallels to *that* student should be obvious. I work with yoga professionals and entrepreneurs who do not really know anything about the law, just like *that* yoga student does not really know anything about asanas or yogic principles. They are copying contracts that do not fit their business, just like the student is modifying asanas that do not fit the student's own body. They are choosing not to use the appropriate documents for aspects of their business, just like the student chooses to skip parts of class that deprive them of the benefits of their efforts. They are using props at the wrong time and in the wrong way with risk of injuring themselves, just as business owners use agreements with provisions they don't understand and bind themselves to agreements that may have an injurious outcome. As yoga teachers, we want to serve our students so they look and feel great. As a yoga lawyer, I want to see our community operate and work healthily and passionately. I'm committed to you not being *that* yoga law client.

Do I Really Need to Work with a Lawyer?

I always get asked whether or not yoga professionals need to work with a lawyer. People will say, "Yeah I get the benefits, but do I really need to do it?" This is a valid question and one that fits in nicely with our discussion of understanding agreements.

The short answer to this question, like any other question that a lawyer will face, is "It depends." It depends on how important it is for you to have the peace of mind of sorting out your business professionally. Do you need an accountant? It depends. It depends how much you care about having your books in order, understanding the financials of your business and getting tax benefits under the direction of a professional. You could just as easily not work with this person and still survive. It is all a personal prerogative.

Let me ask you, do you think some of your students could benefit from private yoga lessons? Would they see a difference in their practice? Could they double their progress if they worked with a teacher who understands their body, and if they did sequences that they specifically need instead of going to group classes twice a week? In most cases, the answer is obviously "yes." But while you see the value of these benefits as a professional yoga teacher, you can appreciate that your friends and potential students may not see it the same way. So, they will continue coming to group classes for years and never get to a level they could potentially reach. And that is okay, *because it is their life and their choice to do so.*

All of this is the same with the law. In fact, I am writing this book on the assumption that you will not be working with a lawyer. I believe that if you learn the lessons in this book, you will be in a much better position than if you did nothing at all. Working with a lawyer on your business is like taking private yoga classes. It is expensive but it makes sense to do it if you believe the benefits are worthwhile. You do not *have* to work with a lawyer to make your business work. Using poor legal documents is the problem and working with a lawyer is not necessarily the panacea. You will be in great shape and may not need to work with a lawyer if you:

1. work with the right people (and know they are the right people);
2. communicate openly and act with integrity;
3. write down your agreements and expectations; and
4. take initiative to learn what you should be doing in your business to protect yourself.

You can do all of these things without a lawyer. One of my friends sold her yoga studio without spending a penny on legal fees. She did her homework and was interested in learning the right way to close the transaction. If you make the effort and have the time and interest, you can learn this stuff too. All I am saying is that using a lawyer is a solution to a problem, and my goal is to create awareness about the problem. The problem is that some people recklessly conduct their business without understanding what they are doing. This will put their relationships and their future at risk. If they can rectify the situation themselves, wonderful. If they need professional help, that is great too. Let's just do what we have to do to get to best practices.

What Should Be Included in an Agreement?

Now that we know it makes sense to have a written agreement, what should we put in the agreement? The terms of an agreement are the different things that people agree on when working together. While the agreement as a whole represents your commitment to the working relationship, the terms make up the specifics of what the working arrangement will look like. Remember that when you sign an agreement, you are agreeing to be *legally bound* to the terms outlined in the agreement. Many of the specific terms in your agreements will vary depending on the nature of the working relationship, but there will also be general things that you will usually agree on with every client.

Think of writing agreements like planning a yoga class. You know what type of asana practice you are planning (i.e. hatha, ashtanga, restorative, etc.) and then you choose a sequence of poses based on a desired outcome. It would not make sense to include every single pose in a class because you will only need a set of poses that enable you to carry out your resolve for that particular class. The same applies to drafting agreements: The type of class is like the type of agreement (waiver, employment agreement, etc.) and the terms (non-compete, release of liability, etc.) are like the asana poses. Once you figure out what your objectives are (like your resolve in planning a yoga class), it is much easier to figure out what you need to include in the agreement.

The following are some things that you will typically find in a business agreement between two parties. Remember that different types of agreements (partnership agreements, waivers of liability, media releases, etc.) have their own specific types of provisions that need to be included. But for the most part, you will always find these general terms in any given agreement:

- Payment – how much is someone paying and when are those payments going to be made? Is there a deposit?

- Services – what specific services will be provided in exchange for the payment?
- Term – how long does the agreement last for?
- Termination – how can the parties end the agreement?
- Property Ownership – if the parties are creating something together, have they decided who will own it?
- Refunds – are refunds permissible if payments are made in advance, or if one party is not satisfied with the services?
- Deadlines – are there deadlines to provide the services, and what happens if deadlines are missed?
- Process – what does the process of working together look like? Who is responsible for what?
- Liability – are the parties seeking to limit their exposure to liability?

As you can see, the terms of an agreement deal with the questions that could arise if there is a problem in the relationship. The idea is that the terms will be able to answer any issue that could arise between the parties. You agree to the terms before the working relationship starts, and then the relationship operates on the understanding that you have already determined what should happen in the event of a disagreement between the parties.

If you plan on drafting your own agreements, think about the "Five W + H" questions: Who, what, where, when, why and how. If your agreement can answer these, you have got a great foundation. You should always think about reading an agreement from the viewpoint of someone who is not involved in the relationship. We call that person an "objective third party." *If there were a dispute in your relationship, would the contract make it clear to an objective third party who is wrong or right, and how the dispute should be resolved?* Always start with the end in mind so that you can anticipate problems and communicate concerns through the terms of your agreement.

Agreements Reflect the Intentions of the Parties

In the first semester of law school, freshly minted law students take a bunch of classes that transform their minds until they start thinking like lawyers. It is sort of like Plato's *The Allegory of the Cave*; once you see what is outside the walls of the cave, you cannot go on pretending like you do not know. In that special first semester of law school, your mind learns to look at everything differently and your entire perspective changes.

All law students must take a class called "Contracts" (perhaps it will be called "Agreements" in the future?) that teaches all the basic aspects of agreements. I could bore you to sleep by going through the content of this class, but I would rather focus on one concept: *Agreements reflect the intentions of the parties making the agreement.* The idea is that what is written in the agreement reflects what the parties intended. If something is omitted from an agreement, the parties presumably chose not to include that particular term. Otherwise, they would have included it, right? This makes sense.

For example: You have your students sign a waiver of liability. The waiver outlines what you will do with the students and it only mentions practicing yoga inside a studio. It does not say anything about doing yoga outdoors or the different risks that students may face if they practice yoga outdoors. When a student reads and signs this agreement, they fairly expect that it only applies to practicing yoga with you indoors. If you wanted them to release you from liability when practicing yoga outdoors or anywhere other than a studio, you would have mentioned it when you asked them to waive their right to legal recourse against you. Right? The presumption is that by not mentioning it, you did not intend for it to be part of the agreement.

Your agreements do not have to outline every single thing that you are expecting from the other party when you work together. Sometimes parties do not expressly say something in an agreement, but the way that the agreement is written could lead someone else to believe that the parties actually intended to agree on that thing. In other words, an obligation can be implied based on the way the parties have agreed to something.

For example, if your agreement says "All teachers must be at the check-in desk fifteen minutes before and fifteen minutes after each class they teach," the presumption is that the teachers will be working during those fifteen minutes before and after class. While the agreement does not expressly state that teachers should be chatting with students and engaging with the community during that time, it could easily be implied. You obviously expect them to be at the desk to hang with students, not to sit on their phones. Such an expectation could easily be implied, even though you did not expressly state it in the agreement.

It is important to understand that in every agreement there are express terms and implied terms. This is important because if you leave something out of your agreement, its absence will appear to be intentional, even if that is not the case. *The starting point is always that you agreed to the terms in the agreement – and if something is not in there, it is not there for a reason.* You may be able to challenge this by saying that the agreement implies you have agreed on a term that is not there, but this will put you in a weaker position than if the term were unequivocally written in the agreement. Remember, you always want to be in control and so clearly expressing what you want in writing will serve you best.

Takeaway: If you do not include a term in an agreement, it is presumed that you did not intend to be bound by such a term. If an agreement is missing a very basic term, you may not get the legal protection of that term unless you can clearly imply its inclusion. For this reason, it is always a good idea to write down in detail everything you expect from the people you work with.

Story: No Refunds

The following is based on a true story that happened to one of my clients. The story illustrates how simple decisions we make about our agreements can have a real impact in our business and our lives. Most of all, it shows how some very simple changes to our existing agreements can make all the difference between stressful, sleepless nights and comfortable success in business and life.

Steve was ambitious, creative and very, very smart. One evening he placed his mat beside mine at One Yoga in Vancouver and we hit it off after class. Initially, we chatted about how much we loved doing yoga with Reno Muenz and how much we loved Ryan Leier. As the conversation went on, it was clear that we loved a lot of the same things. Before I knew it, we were hanging out on Vancouver's Main Street, hiking mountains on the weekend and practicing with our mats beside each other – as brothers do. The most meaningful aspects of life are often found in friendship and personal connection, so I was very glad to have met Steve and have him as part of my life.

After a workout one day, Steve told me a bit about a side hustle he had started, which I thought was quite creative. He had built an online program to connect private yoga teachers with clients seeking private instruction. He was a marketing whiz and knew how to convey his message clearly and to the right people. On top of this, he had been practicing yoga all across North America for years and was very well connected. He had built a landing page, invested in SEO and social media, and then off he went. His business model involved taking a fixed amount for a successful connection between private yoga teachers and his clients. His intentions were beautiful – help out his yogi friends in various cities and provide excellent instructors so that clients could develop their own yoga practices.

We constantly spoke about his business and his dream of using part of the funds from the business to set up an organization that would provide private yoga for at-risk youth. Being such an advocate for private yoga teaching, he felt that everyone was entitled to enjoy such a beautiful practice. I loved what he was doing and was more than happy to be of service.

Steve had been running his business for just less than a year. After I helped him incorporate, we looked at the agreements he was currently using (which he had based on templates downloaded from the Internet). Remember, everything in law is about relationships, so our first step was to see who Steve had business relationships with, and sort them out properly. The independent contractor agreements he had with yoga teachers were subpar but usable. On the other hand, the agreements he had with his paying clients had a plethora of ambiguities. At what point were his services considered fully rendered? What if a client was unsatisfied with the services? Would the fee be a simple one-time payment, or would he continue to collect on it if the client/teacher worked together for certain milestones?

In walking through the agreement with Steve, I learned

what he intended his relationships to look like and realized that the agreement did not fully reflect his expectations. I quickly got to drafting a new client agreement for him and we seemed to have escaped the situation unscathed. He began using the new agreement with his new clients, but he chose not to revisit the original agreements he had with his older clients. "I'm sure everything will be just fine," he said confidently. I advised Steve that he was exposed to some risk if he did not modify his existing agreements, but he made a strategic decision not to rock the boat, and I understood that. As a lawyer, you can advise but you cannot act unless instructed to do so.

The best news of all was that Steve's inner-city private yoga project was gaining momentum. He had been approved for a grant. If he was able to put $10,000 in a bank account dedicated to the project, a government organization would match that amount. It was a highly competitive grant and Steve had three weeks to formally accept it and show that he had the necessary finances. He had just the right amount of money set aside. With the combined $20,000, Steve figured he would be able to provide private yoga classes for one hundred inner-city youth for an entire year – while still paying the teachers fairly, which was very important to him. He texted me the great news and we planned to hang after a yin class to celebrate. Is there any better way than yin yoga to acknowledge the achievement of a major milestone?

One day before we were going to celebrate Steve's massive accomplishment, I saw his name pop up as an incoming call on my phone. "You just couldn't wait until to tomorrow to hear my voice, could you old boy?" I said with a big smile. There was an eerily long pause. "Cory, the project is finished. I'm getting sued. It's all over." I took a deep breath and looked into the bottom of the matcha latte I was holding in my hand. This was not the first time I had picked up the phone hearing those words. "Don't worry bud, it's going to be alright," I said finishing my drink, savouring every last drop. "We'll get through this together," I said confidently. I hopped on my bike and cycled over to meet Steve by the ocean and hear what type of situation we had on our hands.

One of Steve's biggest corporate clients, Andy Lamonte, was not happy with Steve's services and wanted his money back. Plain and simple. Steve had worked quite hard to find nine yoga teachers for Andy's company, and supposedly none of the teachers were working out. Andy had paid the yoga teachers for their time, but now he wanted his money back after apparently spending two months listening to his staff complain about the teachers – teachers not showing up, teachers arriving late, injuries arising out of practice together. Andy's lawyer had sent Steve an email demanding repayment of all amounts paid by Andy to Steve, namely an engagement fee and nine teacher connections totalling $5,500. On top of this, Andy's company sought a damages claim of $1,000 for inconveniences caused. Steve had to pay the full $6,500 within fourteen days, otherwise Andy's company would initiate a lawsuit.

What Steve had received is called a "demand letter." It is a letter that one party uses to begin the negotiations to settle a matter, by providing an amount to be paid and setting a deadline for when that payment should be made. People often misunderstand demand letters under the notion that they are "being sued," which is wholly inaccurate. Negotiations are always a strategic dance back and forth between parties; sending a demand letter is like a chess player making the opening move of the game.

"Andy has basically made the first move and put forward an unrealistic, best possible outcome." I was sitting next to

Steve on a park bench surrounded by trees, looking out to the water of the Georgia Strait. "A demand letter is not being sued – that has to be done through the courts. And demand letters are usually tools to anchor the negotiations and test the other side's willingness to put up a fight." Andy looked at me and asked, "What is anchoring?" I explained that an anchor is a number or range of numbers that people choose to start negotiations. The idea is that one side chooses a number to anchor your expectations, which they hope will set the course for the negotiations. "So if Andy would be happy to settle with $2,000, $5,500 is a good starting point because if we settle at $2,500, you will think that you have gotten a good deal. When in fact, you would still be overpaying."

As I was explaining this concept, I remembered a story that Steve had told me about a trip he once took to Myanmar. "Remember when you were in Myanmar and you took that hot air balloon in Bagan?" I saw a twinkle in Steve's eye and a faint smile for the first time since the bad news broke. "You told me that they originally wanted $550, but in the end you negotiated your way down to $400? Well, most certainly, they would have been thrilled to get $350. It was only by inflating the first price that they made you feel content with a number that still meant you would be overpaying." Steve looked at me, finally starting to get it. "All that is happening here is that Andy is starting negotiations off with an inflated number, so that if I settle for less, he will say that he is being reasonable and that I am getting a good deal." Exactly.

On top of this, I told Steve that in a demand letter, the other side will often make outlandish allegations. They will manipulate facts to make their case seem air-tight and totally unchallengeable. This little trick often trips clients up. "We've lost, we have no chance," they will say. But again, such arguments just set the stage for the negotiations to follow – and only those who are well versed in negotiations really get this. "You can't take anything in that letter seriously. It's like a kid writing up a list of what they want for Christmas. They are painting a picture in an unrealistic world where they are totally in the right and everything that could go their way, will. Although the situation is serious, we don't have to take their initial position too seriously because it will inevitably change."

The most important thing, I told Steve, was that everything would be fine. "I go through this all the time with clients, you don't have to sweat it bro. As hard as it will be, just try to relax and know that I've got your back and I've done this many times before. I'll just draft a response to Andy's lawyer and we'll get the ball rolling." Steve heard me but looked as pale as a ghost. Clearly, he was not going to be able to rest with his monkey mind racing through thoughts of being sued and the project he worked so hard for hanging in the balance. "The project... the kids... the grant," he muttered under his breath. "It's all good buddy, everything will go ahead as planned. You have my word." I told Steve that we would be in touch, and with that, we parted ways.

I drafted a reply and sent it to Steve. I explained that everything seemed magnified and more serious than it really was because he had no experience in dealing with these matters. Andy's side would make allegations and threats, and we would make allegations and threats – but in the end, after assessing the legal strength of both positions, we would collectively end up at a number that worked for both sides and it would all be over. This is how it happens most of the time. Steve just had to meditate, believe and trust that everything would be fine.

With Steve's approval, I sent a reply to Andy's team saying that Steve had completed the services. Steve had been hired to provide Andy with yoga teachers for his company and had done so. As such, he would not be making any payment. Further, the claim for damages was unsubstantiated and could not be proven, so the $6,500 was inflated and unrealistic. The response said that we were open to resolving the matter without further escalation and were looking forward to a reply. Just as Andy's note was ceremonious in the sense that it just had to get the ball rolling, our reply was equally indirect and fanciful. After sending the reply, I made my way to the law library to begin researching the strength of our case.

Luckily for Steve's sanity and sleeping patterns, things began to move quickly towards a resolution. This was good for us, because Steve was under time pressure to match the government grant. The other side did not know this piece of information, which was fortunate because it would have significantly changed the negotiating dynamics. After a series of exchanges back and forth between the sides, and after I had completed my research on our legal position, we finally got to the "negotiation" aspect of the negotiations. The crux of the issue was this: *The agreement did not say that there would be no refunds for payments made by Andy to Steve.* Further, because Steve had downloaded a basic agreement from the Internet that was not related to his business, it would be difficult to make an argument that the parties had implied all payments to be full and final.

Andy's argument was that he had hired Steve to provide yoga teachers that he and his team would be satisfied with – and until Steve had completed that job, Andy should not have to pay him a penny. This was not the best argument that I had come up against, but the problem was that *Andy was right in principle*. If it was Steve's intention to not offer refunds based on the quality of the services he provided, he should have said so. It was difficult to explain this to Steve when we met up for a lift.

"So, you're telling me that if my agreement had included two small words, No Refunds, this problem would just go away?" I made sure to keep eye contact and then replied, "Yeah man, it sorta sucks but at least you're learning this lesson at a relatively cheap cost." Steve was distraught. "I won't get the government grant and my program will never get off the ground. I haven't slept in a week and all I can think about is getting sued." He almost screamed in frustration. "I'm stressed about everything in my life right now, I just want this to end." I got out of my seat and motioned for him to stand up, then slowly moved my arms to surround his body and pulled him in close. I gave him a hug. The human side of the law is so often neglected. "I understand what you are going through and it will be alright. I promise you it will be alright." Steve held on tight and then abruptly let go. "I've got to get the government grant sorted in the next couple of days, so please try to end this soon," he pleaded. I was on the case.

To understand how the rest of the negotiations went, and why they went the way they did, there is one important thing to understand about negotiations: *Unless someone has a slam-dunk, homerun, absolute winning case (which would still be shrouded in some uncertainty), no one really wants to go court.* This is why so many cases settle outside of court, and thus why so few people actually resolve their lawsuits in front of a judge. When you go to court, you get put in front of a judge who may or may not buy your side of the story. That element of risk – the risk that the judge will not agree with your arguments on that particular day – is terrifying. Losing sucks. Losing and paying legal fees for a full-blown trial is even worse.

I knew Andy and his team had no intention of going to

small claims court, and that this issue, like so many problems, *wasn't really about the money.* It was about some sort of principle. It was my job to find out what was at the bottom of all of this. Nothing is ever as it seems in negotiations. After hopping on a call with Andy's lawyer and participating in some active listening, I was able to see that the issue was about a few things – frustration, wasted time, disappointment and misaligned expectations. This was a positive development because it showed that we could offer things besides money that could help resolve the problem. As a rule of thumb: If someone is asking for money, they usually really want something else.

Steve and I sat down and spoke about the different ways we could find a way to please Andy while minimizing the out-of-pocket cost to his program. In the end, we drafted a solution that included an apology (you would be amazed how far the words *I'm sorry* can go), a promise to find replacement teachers and a nominal fee to acknowledge the challenges that Andy had gone through. In exchange, Andy would agree not to bring any further actions against Steve in the future.

Once we had finalized the offer, Steve looked at me and said, "I'm livid." I could see the anger in his eyes. "I don't want to do this. I shouldn't have to do this. Screw this guy," he said, slamming his fist into his hand. "Steve," I said, "if we can get rid of this problem and make sure you have enough money for your program, then we win. We're in a tight spot and you'll win when this is over and children get private yoga classes from the amazing work you've done. We're super close." Steve mulled this over for a second and then a faint smile emerged on his face, the edges of his lips turning upwards. "Alright, get it done," he said.

I got back to Andy's lawyer with our proposal and a hard deadline. I included Steve's written apology for Andy before sending the proposal, which seemed to go a long way. Andy's lawyer responded that Andy would accept the nominal payment and sign the document agreeing not take any further action against Steve in the future. I received back the signed copy of our offer and instructed Steve to pay $500 to Andy's lawyer via a bank draft. Once payment was confirmed, I printed everything, kept it for our records and texted Steve to meet up because I had good news.

Steve was finishing up a private yoga class with one of the kids in his program. I could see him closing the lesson with a few *aum* chants and made my way over. His radiant and electric energy had returned. He greeted me with a smile. "Here you go brother," I said and handed him the documents. He extended his hand to shake mine. "Well that sucked," he said candidly. "It did," I agreed with a giggle, "but it's over now. You got away nearly unscathed and resolved this quickly. Imagine if this was for more money, with a bigger jerk, and was dragged out for years." He responded immediately: "Nope, I don't want to imagine that." We both laughed.

As we started leaving the practice space, the kid from Steve's private class screamed, "Hey wait for me." We had both forgot about him as he was rolling up his mat on the ground, drunk in our gaiety from the recently solved dispute. "That was a great class Steve, but it wasn't long enough," the kid said. "I wanted to do handstands for longer and we didn't even get to do any yoga nidra. Not fair, I want my money back," he pouted.

Steve and I looked at each other with the same silly smile on our face, and at the same time we blurted out, "NO REFUNDS," dying in laughter. The kid looked confused and embarrassed for us. He ran ahead with his yoga mat in hand and called back, "Whatever, you guys are weird."

Your Chapter Checklist

If you remember nothing else, be sure to grasp and apply these concepts:

- Agreements form the basis of your relationships in business. When you sign an agreement, you are legally bound to its terms.
- Using agreements that you don't understand can be dangerous, because you are agreeing to something that you don't fully comprehend and can cause trouble for you in the future.
- Agreements reflect the intentions of the people signing the agreement. If something is excluded, it is presumed that you meant to exclude it.
- There are simple things to include in your agreements, like a "No Refunds" clause which can save you a lot of money and headaches. The types of provisions you will need in your agreement will depend on the type of business you are doing and who you are doing it with.

Chapter 4

Choosing Your Posture: Corporate Structures + Setting up Your Business

Intention

Our goal in this chapter is to outline the different options you have when deciding how to structure your business. By going through the different structures one by one, it should become clear which option would suit you best. I will explain how each structure is unique and then go through the pros and cons of each choice, with examples of how it could apply to your business. I will also share stories that highlight the importance of solidifying your structure with the proper partnership agreement or shareholder agreement. Choosing the right structure is important for tax and liability purposes, not to mention your control of the business. You also have to consider what personal assets and debts you have, and what assets and debts your partners may have as well.

If you remember only one thing from this chapter, remember that whatever organizational structure you choose, there is a full process to complete in setting up your business that way. I have noticed that most of my clients have no difficulty making a choice, but a high percentage of them do not solidify the relationship properly. It does not serve you, your business or anyone you work with to incorporate but not have a shareholder agreement, or to establish a partnership but not sign a partnership agreement. Whatever you do, do it right.

Choose Your Resolve

Before any discussion of corporate structures, you need to come up with a resolve for your business. That is, *why are you doing this?* Is your goal to add a bit of side income into your life and secure teaching gigs at your favourite studio? Or do you have a killer idea for a new studio that you want to put in major cities across the globe? Are you working alone or do you want to work with others? Do you have money to finance the project, or are you looking to raise money once you get into business? These are just a few of the questions that you should consider when deciding which structure would fit you best.

Later, in Chapter 7, I will write about the importance of reverse engineering your business. The idea is that you should think about where you want your business to end up and then simply work backwards. Every decision you make relating to your business must be aligned with your end goals. It is much easier to know how to design your business when you are clear about where you want to take it – i.e. are you building it to sell it, or do you plan on using it to support your livelihood and family?

This seems like a good opportunity for you to think a little bit about your business goals and where you want to take your business. Feel free to take a break and journal some of this out, get into a juicy meditation, start manifesting, or go for a run and think about what you are really looking for in starting this endeavour. Think about the following questions:

- How important is it that you work alone or with others?
- Will your business have employees, and if so, will you motivate them with the possibility of ownership in the company one day?
- Is making money the most important aspect of your business?

- Where is the business in one, three and five years – and where are you in one, three and five years?
- How much money do you forecast making in your first year and how much do you forecast making in your third year?
- Are you operating a business with a high exposure to risk?
- Do you have personal assets (a car, a home, etc.) that you would like to protect?

Take some time to get clear on your answers and then go through the rest of this chapter with your direction in mind. One type of business structure should speak to you more than others.

Overarching Principles

There are a couple of basic principles that will continuously pop their head up as we discuss different corporate structures. I am going to spell them out here very simply so that you get the concepts and can refer back to them. You will want to consider the following things when choosing a corporate structure, in concert with your personal and professional goals – the liability of your business, the protection of your personal assets and the amount you will pay in taxes. I will touch on the overarching principles gently.

Liability + Personal Assets

In this context, just understand the following equation: Liability = your responsibility for something. The law chooses different scenarios in which you will be responsible for someone or something, whether you like it or not. For example, when you lead someone in a yoga class, you have a responsibility to make sure that person will be fine while they are in your care (at a minimum).

Liability is an important concept in choosing a corporate structure because it is possible that your choice of structure will make you *personally liable* for your business relationships. Being personally liable means that you, as a person, will be responsible for paying back anything owed, lost or suffered in the course of business. Even worse, your personal assets (i.e. your car, your home, your savings) can be taken from you to satisfy any debts that you incur on behalf of the business. In a partnership, you will be personally liable not only for your own debts but also the debts of your partner.

However, personal liability is not an issue if your business is a separate legal entity. A separate legal entity is something that is created and recognized as being different from the people who create it. The separate entity can enter into its own business agreements and will be liable for its own actions. The benefit is that even though you may be involved in a company as a shareholder (an owner of the company) and a director (someone who helps run the company), you will not be personally liable for the debts and liabilities of the company. Your personal assets are safe – and in a worst-case scenario, the company declares bankruptcy and the buck normally stops there.

Examples of separate legal entitles are: Companies, LLCs, registered charities, non-profits and cooperatives. Examples of structures where personal liability applies and there is NO separate legal entity are: Sole proprietorships and partnerships.

Taxes

There are only three things guaranteed in the life of a professional yogi – pranayama, sivasana and taxes.

The amount of money your business must pay in taxes each year will depend on which legal structure you choose. This is because the government sets different tax rates for businesses and other organizational structures. Taxes are not my speciality – and to be honest, this is not an area that I know too much about – so I normally work with some amazing accountants. I would recommend that anyone starting a business find an awesome accountant who can answer questions and offer valuable advice about organizational structures. There are a million different ways that one can use taxes to support a business and lifestyle while complying with civil duties to governmental organizations.

Here is the main thing that I want you to know: *Just as there are legal ramifications in selecting an organizational structure, there are also tax implications.* A lawyer can help you with the legal decisions and an accountant can help you with the tax questions. Building a dream team of professionals that you respect and feel comfortable working with is one of the most FUN aspects of business. Adding an accountant to the team is super helpful, especially when choosing the type of business you will run.

Things to Keep in Mind

Now that you understand the overarching principles, you will want to keep the following questions in mind as you learn more about the different structures and how they may apply to you:

1. Do I have personal assets that I would place at risk by not creating a separate legal entity?
2. Is my business so "high-risk" that liability becomes an issue and there is a chance I will be personally responsible to pay off debts incurred by the business?
3. From a big picture perspective, what are the tax implications of running my business as a company versus running it as an individual taxpayer?

First Pose: Operating a Sole Proprietorship

A sole proprietorship is a fairly straightforward option. All it means is that you are operating the business as yourself and are personally responsible for the business's liabilities and debts. You can easily register your sole proprietorship in the province/ state where you live. You apply to register your business under a chosen business name, and then once you are registered you can begin carrying on your business under that name. When you sign agreements for the business, you can sign either as yourself personally or as the name of the registered sole proprietorship.

There are some important benefits to choosing this structure. There is no cost to set up a sole proprietorship; there is minimal upkeep of the business; and there are no governmental obligations for filing or keeping the business in good standing. The business itself is not taxed and all of the money gets passed through the sole proprietor individually. However, the biggest concern to keep in mind when operating a sole proprietorship is that you are personally responsible for all debts and liabilities of the business. The appropriate legal agreements can help to mitigate liabilities and risk. Insurance also plays a huge part because you want to make sure that there is a buffer between your business and your assets. But of course, insurance has its own complications.

Examples of When a Sole Proprietorship Makes Sense

Example #1: My accountant Jason (a wonderful fellow whom I have never met but always speak to on the phone) advised me that I should set up Conscious Counsel as a sole proprietorship and not a corporation. There were three main reasons for this. First, when I started the business I was not earning enough to warrant incorporation. Second, the Law Society provides insurance to all lawyers for coverage in professional practice. Third, I did not have personal assets and so I was exposed to little risk. Being a sole proprietor made the most sense for me.

Example #2: I had a most wonderful client who started a business making a particular type of yoga socks. She was passionate about knitting, had unique designs and most importantly was enthusiastic about her work. It made sense for her to start as a sole proprietor and her accountant agreed, for the following reasons. Her business was not going to grow very much in its first year. She sourced the materials herself and her legal relationships were limited to the agreements that she had to fulfil with distributors. We used a "no refund" clause for her products and let's face it, *there is little risk involved with selling socks.*

Example #3: Most of my yoga teacher clients have good insurance and do not earn enough to incorporate, so operating as a sole proprietor makes sense for them. Yoga is not a very risky business to operate (compared to the heli-skiing clients I have worked with in the past), and one can protect oneself from liability with a solid waiver and a few other strategic approaches. I always ask these clients to communicate with an accountant to corroborate this assessment, and they usually end up taking the route of sole proprietorship, especially when starting off.

Takeaway: If you have no major personal assets, operate a low-risk enterprise, protect yourself with insurance, use appropriate legal documents and get the blessing of an accountant, a sole proprietorship could be your best bet.

Second Pose: Partnerships

Partnerships are lovely, they really are. They provide a platform for two or more people to work together and build something amazing. I always think of partnerships like marriages or other long-term relationships that need to be strong enough to withstand the tests of time and life's ups and downs. Just as parents bring a child into the world, partners bring their unique business into the world, raising it to reach its potential and make a difference for others.

In the legal context, you can think of a partnership as a sole proprietorship with more than one person. How fun, what a party! However, a partnership does have its own nuances that are important to understand before you grab someone's hand, get down on one knee and take the leap. From my experience working with clients in partnership, the most important thing to understand is the following point: *The liabilities and assets of a partnership are shared between the parties.* This means that all partners share the profits of the partnership and are personally responsible to pay off the debts of the partnership. This is a critical concept to grasp because it can lead to a whole suite of issues.

Here are just *some* examples of situations when a partnership can give rise to issues:
- When one partner does more work than the other, but they get paid equally.
- When a partner incurs debt on behalf of the partnership

without the approval of the other partner, who is now responsible for paying it back.

- When partners have different views on how the business should be run.
- When one partner wants to sell the business and the other does not.
- When the partnership is ending and the partners want to determine who owns what moving forwards.

As a lawyer, some of the most common problems that I deal with in dispute resolution arise from partnerships. For this reason, I am going to break down some of the major issues that arise in partnerships below. But do not worry – things are not all doom and gloom. Being in a partnership can be lovely and there are simple ways to rectify problems before they come up. One point that I will come back to is the *importance of signing a partnership agreement*. It is so important to communicate expectations in a partnership agreement before starting a partnership. It may suck to have an uncomfortable conversation, but there is nothing more important you can do for your business.

Partnership Issue #1: Personal and Joint Sharing of Assets + Liabilities

The first issue to understand about partnerships relates to liability and ownership. Firstly, a partnership is not a separate legal entity, but rather two or more people carrying on business personally. This means that the partners are personally liable for the debts and liabilities of the partnership. Secondly, the partners *jointly share* those assets and liabilities of the business. What does that mean? There are a few different nuances that I will explain as simply as possible.

Joint sharing of assets means that partners are equally entitled to all assets of the partnership, unless agreed otherwise. If they do not agree anything to the contrary, the partners will split all of the money and property of the partnership. Everything created by the partnership belongs to the partnership. So if one partner is doing all of the work in the partnership and creates something amazing that becomes a smash hit, the property of the creation belongs to... wah wah... the partnership. Partnerships are great when both partners contribute equally on behalf of the partnership, but they are a drag when one person is doing all of the work.

On the flip side, and this is juicy: Partners are *jointly* liable for the debts and liabilities of the partnership. If one partner incurs a debt or gets sued on behalf of the partnership and cannot cover the cost, the other partner will be personally responsible for settling it. This is why it is usually good to get to know a potential partner quite well before going into partnership together. In law school, I read some classic cases where one partner duped the other partner into entering a partnership, only to take a loan out on behalf of the partnership and then skip town, leaving the other unfortunate soul to foot the bill.

Partnership Issue #2: Break-Ups and the Importance of Partnership Agreements

I do a funny exercise in my Yoga Law lectures where I discuss the topic of partnerships by talking about a break-up. I invite someone onto the stage to tell a story about when they were in love. I will ask, "What was it like at the start?" and the answer is always, "It was perfect. We were planning to spend the rest of our lives together." I will wait for a moment and then ask,

"What was it like at the end?" At this point I will get a bunch of different answers that all end the same way. Relationships end. No judgement, they just do. A very small percentage of relationships do not end. And this is a beautiful thing.

The point is that everyone has been in a relationship that ended. I once hopped on a plane to Hawaii to visit a girl for a week, and if you had asked me right then whether I thought it would work out, I would have said, "Yes." I wouldn't have gone to Hawaii if I hadn't thought it would work out. Four days. FOUR DAYS. That's how long it lasted.

Have a think about this: Business relationships are just another kind of relationship. Think about your most ridiculous or serious break-up. How did you feel at the start of the relationship? How did you feel at the end? Now, can you imagine reaching the end and having to decide how to divide your corporate baby, your years of hard work, your passion and your livelihood? Humans are complex and our complexity is only magnified when we are doing something as complex as running a business.

I am not a fear monger. I'm an optimist. I believe in soul mates. I believe in true love. But I will do everything in my power to encourage partners to sign a partnership agreement. A good partnership agreement can resolve most of the issues and problems that come up in a partnership. The agreement will set out how the partnership will run, who will be responsible for doing what, and how the partnership can be dissolved if one or both of the partners seek to end the relationship. This literally sets the rules for how to play the game and how to end it. Imagine if you had to play a game like Connect Four without rules… madness!

I would encourage you to reverse engineer your business when working with the law (see Chapter 7) and partnerships are no different. Starting with the end in mind is a great way to determine why you are starting the partnership, where you want to take it and what issues could come up in the future. Yes, it is difficult to have a conversation about breaking up your partnership, but trust me that it is so much better to have this conversation while partners are on good terms with each other. A partnership agreement is like the pre-nup of corporate law. The story below illustrates the challenges of dissolving a partnership when the partners are not getting along and have not signed a partnership agreement.

Partnership Story: Yoga Retreat Partners Break Up

Wendy was one of my first friends when I moved to Vancouver. At the time, she was starting her professional yoga practice as a teacher and I would regularly drop into her classes. What made Wendy's classes unique was her ability to be truly present in the room. She would just walk in and share something about herself or how she was feeling and have it land in a perfectly relatable way for everyone in the room. Magic! What a gift! She changed my life on numerous occasions.

As my friendship with Wendy grew over time, so did Wendy's yoga following. She transitioned from teaching at smaller studios to teaching in the prime spots at any studio she liked. She ran her first retreat by herself, developed a strong following online and was being asked to serve as a faculty member for teacher trainings. The stars were aligning for wonderful Wendy.

One day, Wendy was approached by a retreat organizer named Cheryl who had a beautiful retreat space on Salt Spring Island, a very special place in the Canadian Southern Gulf Islands. Cheryl had been looking to fill the retreat space with trendy yoga teachers who could put her location on the map. She had also been working with a yoga teacher from Costa Rica named Rodrigo who she believed could bring in the international crowds. From the outset, all three of them – Wendy, Cheryl and Rodrigo – seemed to have all their bases covered: A beautiful yoga space, a local teacher and an international teacher. What could go wrong?

Because you have made it this far in the book, you are probably jumping out of your seat thinking: SIGN AGREEMENTS, COMMUNICATE EXPECTATIONS and HAVE DIFFICULT CONVERSATIONS. You are definitely onto something. Partnerships usually work smoothly at the start because everyone loves each other and is so excited for the project. But as a partnership picks up momentum and things start happening, challenges pop up and partners learn things about each other's working styles or character traits that they did not know before. This is precisely when agreements are needed to keep people in check and accountable.

As you might imagine, our three amigos Wendy, Cheryl and Rodrigo had little experience in working with the law. They dove head-first into their new project (a good thing) without reaching any form of partnership agreement (a bad thing). First they started building a brand and designed a logo. They built a website and chose a name for the monthly retreats they would run: "The Journey Home: Yoga Retreats to Rediscover Your True Self." They each contributed assets of varying amounts without formally documenting the contributions or outlining any form of re-payment. They did not create a budget, coordinate their expenses or set up a partnership bank account. There was no agreement on how partners were expected to act or how one partner could be removed from the partnership.

The next part of the story should come as no surprise to

you. It didn't take long for the partners to see that they were not contributing equally to the partnership – both financially and in terms of their effort – and that they really did not work well together. They had been brought together by "serendipitous circumstances" facilitated "by the Universe" and had never tried out what it would be like to work together. It was clear that Rodrigo was not all he was cracked up to be. He focused most of his attention on the retreats he was running in Costa Rica, never attended meetings and racked up expenses that the group had never agreed to. For the first retreat, the trio had signed up fourteen attendees – ten signed by Wendy, four by Cheryl and none by Rodrigo. When all was said and done, the partners split their profits evenly, which seemed grossly unfair to Wendy and Cheryl. During a late meeting one night, Wendy and Cheryl agreed that Rodrigo had to go.

The next day, Wendy was teary-eyed as she asked me how she could get out of the mess. She wanted to keep her legal fees low but salvage the business that she loved and relied on. I asked her a few questions and realized that legally the odds were not in our favour. The problem was that Wendy, Cheryl and Rodrigo had entered into their partnership equally and now shared the business evenly between them (since they had not agreed otherwise). Also, they did not have an agreement on how things should end, so there was no process for kicking out one of the partners from the partnership. The situation was dire because Rodrigo was a rightful owner of everything they had worked on – branding, content, mailings lists, etc. – and it would have been illegal to deprive him of the benefits of that work.

I told Wendy that she would have to resolve the problem as a real person first, with the support of the law second. We would be okay if she and Cheryl could chat with Rodrigo and find a workable solution that dissolved his participation in the partnership. And as things go sometimes, it was not too difficult to do this. At first Rodrigo was very hurt and refused to let go. However, I coached Wendy (as I do with other clients) to play detective during her negotiations with the other party: What is the person really saying? What can you learn about their feelings from what they are sharing with you? After many meetings, Wendy learned that Rodrigo was attached to being a "Co-founder" of the retreat because he felt that it helped leverage his brand in Costa Rica. He was not interested in receiving a share of the revenues or running the retreats on Salt Spring. He cared about the spotlight and how he could use it to help his image.

So, easily enough, we drafted a partnership separation agreement that would let Rodrigo keep the title of Co-founder with no other entitlements. Everyone agreed, we signed the agreement and the crisis was averted. Sometimes a problem will get resolved this easily, but it rarely does. Rodrigo could have held out for more money or forced his partners to stop operating under their brand and start from scratch. This was a good reminder that in law and in life, you never want a situation to be out of your own control. Act first, act prudently, and communicate intentions openly and honestly, so that you can ensure your relationships will serve your life and your business.

Takeaway: There are consequences to starting a partnership (shared assets and liabilities), and it is difficult to get out of the partnership if you do not have a partnership agreement – especially if you want to continue the business without a current partner. You will pour your heart, soul and energy into your business, so you owe it to yourself to ensure that you have important mechanisms in place before you start, including a process for dissolving the partnership.

Third Pose: Limited Liability Companies

Limited Liability Company or an "LLC" is a very common form of business structure for entrepreneurs and small business owners in the United States. In Canada, LLCs do not exist. Part of what makes LLCs so desirable is that they offer the benefits of the corporate protection (i.e. your personal assets are not at risk) as a separate legal entity and also offer flexibility when it comes to tax strategies. An LLC can have as many owners (called "Members") as desired, with a minimum of at least one. It is a hybrid of a corporation and a partnership all rolled into one, hence its popularity amongst small business owners.

Fourth Pose: Incorporation + Shareholder Agreements

The big takeaway is that incorporation is the creation of a separate legal entity. You fill out some forms online and – *viola*! – the government recognizes your company as a corporation that is separate from you. You may be a director or shareholder of your company, but you are not your company. There is a difference. And this difference is what limits the liability of your commercial operations to your company and not you personally. In law school this concept is explained by calling the company "a corporate shield." The separate legal entity serves as a shield to protect you and your personal assets from the operations of the business. This is why many people incorporate a company.

There are many other reasons why people choose to incorporate a company. Incorporation can save you a lot of money from a tax perspective, especially if you are able to leave money in the company and not pay out all profits as dividends (again, your accountant will advise you best). Also, when you incorporate you can issue shares in the company, which represent a piece of ownership in the company. There are different types of shares: Common shares, preferential shares, voting shares, non-voting shares. If you are looking to raise money for your business and would like to do so privately (instead of taking a bank loan), it can be a great idea to have the flexibility of issuing shares in exchange for capital.

For our purposes, we will be in great shape if you can grasp the following concepts:

1. Incorporating a company creates a separate legal entity. This means that you and your business are not the same thing (unlike in a sole proprietorship or a partnership). This in turn limits the liability of your business operations to your company, so that you are not personally liable for the company's actions, debts and liabilities.

2. There can be significant tax advantages to incorporating a company, but the numbers have to be right. Consult with your accountant for more details.

3. When you incorporate a company, you can issue shares (ownership) to other people. This allows you to raise money for your business in exchange for others owning a part of the business, which can be a wonderful and easy way to raise money without having to pay it back plus interest.

Below is a story that highlights one of the benefits of incorporation: The protection that comes with entering into agreements on behalf of a company as a separate legal entity. One of my clients was able to protect her personal assets by signing a lease through her company and not signing it personally.

Incorporation Story #1: Corporate Liability Saves the Day

One of my clients approached me with a bit of an issue. She owned a yoga studio that was failing and her efforts to keep it going were draining her. The studio was losing money and she had to fight each month just to pay her staff, pay the landlord and cover other expenses of running the business. She had a young daughter and was upset with how little time she was able to spend with her family. So, she decided to fold the business and needed some help in reaching that goal.

We gathered all of my client's agreements (luckily she had most of them in order) and went through them to decide how to properly wrap things up. We learned how much notice she had to give to terminate all of her relationships with teachers, students and other service providers at the studio. However, when we looked at how to end the lease, things were less clear. The lease did not have a termination option and my client was only in the eighth month of a three-year term. The lease was silent on what would happen in the event of bankruptcy or my client going broke and out of business.

I reached out to my client's landlord with an olive branch to see what we could arrange for a win/win scenario, but this guy was not in the mood to play nice. When I mentioned that it was more than likely my client would declare bankruptcy and be unable to pay, the landlord responded in an irate tone: "I'll get my money even if I have to go after her personally. And, I know her husband has money, I looked into it before she signed the lease."

My client was obviously rattled and terrified when I relayed this message back to her. But luckily, the legal entity that had signed the lease was her company and not her personally. Further, she had not provided a personal guarantee on the lease (in other words, she had not agreed to use personal assets to back up the company in the event that it was unable to pay what it owed, which is not uncommon in a lease). This meant that the company was the only entity responsible for fulfilling the obligations of the contract.

This was a major relief because once the company declared bankruptcy and showed that it had no money or means to fulfill its responsibilities in the contract, the landlord was unable to seek recourse against my client personally. She had acted properly and professionally. Declaring bankruptcy had broken her heart, but luckily she had protected her personal assets from this unfortunate circumstance by signing the lease through her company and not signing a personal guarantee.

Shareholder Agreements: What Are They and Why Do You Need Them?

An incorporated company is owned by the people who hold the shares of the company, known as the shareholders. There is a document – an oh-so-special document – called a shareholder agreement that plays a crucial role in explaining the rules of how the company's ownership will work. Here are some examples of the different issues that a shareholder agreement can address:

- How often should shareholders be paid out from the company's profits, and in what amount?
- What happens if one of the shareholders dies or becomes incapacitated?
- What processes are required to sell the business if an offer is made?

- What is the process for bringing on new owners or partners for the business?
- How should the resources of the business be used, and how should they not be used?

A shareholder agreement can also set rules for how the company will make decisions and operate itself. When you operate a sole proprietorship or a partnership, it is easy for the company to make decisions because you and your company are one and the same. But once you create a separate legal entity through incorporation, there needs to be a process for making decisions on behalf of that entity. Typically, incorporated companies are run and operated by officers and directors who must act in the best interest of the company.

So, the intention of a shareholder agreement is to outline how an incorporated company should be run and how important decisions about the company should be made. If you are the only shareholder in the company, you do not really have to worry about this because you have no one to answer to but yourself and can do whatever you want with the business as long as it is legal. However, if there are other shareholders in the company (especially if there are shareholders with different types of shares – called "classes" of shares), then you will definitely need a shareholder agreement to set rules around the company's ownership and operation.

Shareholder agreements are by far the most complex documents I work with. They are usually the ones that clients find most intimidating, because they are long, thorough and raise a lot of uncomfortable issues. Unsurprisingly, clients have given me lots of reasons for why they do not need a shareholder agreement. Some classic reasons are that "we are best friends and would never have a fight," and that "we totally have the same vision for the company and don't need to pay $1,600 to organize that." I get it, I really do. When people start a business, they love each other. They are so high on the rush of doing something they have always wanted to do that they feel and believe everything will work out. Perfect. I love this and do not want to be a party pooper by any means. Anyone who knows me knows that I love celebrating every chance I get.

That being said, you can love your business partner, share the same vision for everything business-related AND sign an agreement that outlines the rules for running your business. Doing so *only makes things easier in the future*. This is because you will fight and you will disagree and you will need a document that reminds you of what your intentions were when you started the business. A shareholder agreement is about being mature and treating your business like… a business.

I once had a client who went into business with his best friend. "No way, we don't need to pay for a shareholder agreement now," he told me. "We need to get clients first." I replied with all the reasons why having a shareholder agreement makes sense, including the unpredictability of life and the need to know that families will be taken care of fairly should an accident ever happen. I was shunned and shut down. Although I was not personally upset, I did want the best for my client. A week later, however, I got a surprise phone call from him. "I was an inch away from getting hit by a bus yesterday. I want to sign a shareholder agreement tomorrow." And, sometimes it works like this.

At the start of this chapter, I said that if you remember only one thing then you should remember to fully commit to your chosen organizational structure by solidifying it and doing it right. Committing to a shareholder agreement helps you avoid what I call "The Abyss." The Abyss is a situation where parties enter a legal relationship that has no pre-determined next step, and thereby leave the pathways for resolving an issue shrouded in mist, uncertainty, stress – and heavy financial cost.

If parties build a thriving business without a shareholder agreement, and then decide that someone wants out – or that one person wants to bring on a new partner, or that they disagree on a fundamental aspect of the business, or that they now hate each other – they are stuck in The Abyss. They did not agree beforehand about how issues should be resolved or how they must act in certain scenarios. As a result, they will hire lawyers, waste lots of money, continue floating in conflict and get distracted from their business. And this breaks my heart. Building a successful business is the hard part; organizing your relationship is the easy part. I hate when people have this the other way around.

I am not asking you to be perfect, but I am asking you to be responsible. The dominant principle in this book is the importance of communicating expectations in your relationships. Think of this like your breath in yoga. You cannot do yoga if you do not breathe. You cannot hold poses if you do not breathe. You cannot be centered if you do not breathe. So too in law, you cannot have a healthy or heart-leading business without communicating expectations in your relationships. A shareholder agreement is one of the most important ways to communicate expectations for an incorporated company, and so I urge you to draft one with your fellow owners that appropriately reflects the intentions and values of the company.

Incorporation Story #2: When Shareholder Agreements Work

I want to share this happy story about one of my clients who signed a shareholder agreement right after she incorporated her business, and then was able to use it to save her relationship with her business partner and find a clear path for moving forward.

I received an email one day from Karen, a client who was organized and knew exactly what she was looking for. She had done her homework and was ready to get the ball rolling. I met Karen and her business partner Levi for a coffee right after an amazing Sunday-morning class with Kate Gillespie, one of my favourite yoga teachers in Vancouver. I was in my post-savasana bliss zone when I hugged the pair and told them how happy I was to help out. After a few minutes of small talk and getting to know one another, I was presented with a well-organized and colour-coordinated binder containing all of the information I would need to draft their shareholder agreement.

As a lawyer, I sometimes work with clients who know everything about the law and are extremely prepared, and other times I work with clients who have no idea what they are looking for or what they need. Karen and Levi were certainly the former. I loved reviewing their business plan, learning why they loved what they were doing and seeing how clear they were on their legal and professional obligations to each other. Karen and Levi planned on building a business around outdoor yoga experiences, specifically weekend yoga camping trips and excursions. They planned to sell yoga-themed outdoor equipment and expand into the corporate market, offering retreats and team-building exercises in nature. I loved everything about their plan.

After reviewing their folder, we began a conversation that I usually have with shareholders before I draft an agreement. The conversations usually cover the following topics:

- Would Karen and Levi be equal partners and hold equal shares?

- Would either partner invest money to set up the business, and what would be the process for the company repaying them for their investment?
- What would constitute a major decision that they would need to run by each other, and what would be a minor decision they could make independently? (For example, we agreed that any expenditure over $500 was a major decision, and that managing Instagram posts was a minor decision.)
- Did they plan to bring on any other shareholders, and if so, what would the process be for determining how to do this?
- What entitlements would their partners or common law partners have in the business in the event of a divorce or separation?
- What would happen in the event of a shareholder's death or incapacitation?
- Would either shareholder be allowed to work for another company that was in competition with the business?
- How could they end the relationship and what would happen if one partner wanted out?

These conversations are never easy because they require you to plan how the company will facilitate a break-up of the owners. But as I have mentioned earlier in this book, sometimes the most difficult conversations are the most important ones to have. You confront ghosts and parade elephants directly into the middle of the room. I have seen amazing things happen when business partners speak openly and honestly with each other about their expectations. And I can tell you this: Almost every single time that I have facilitated shareholder conversations, the end result is a more positive situation than when we started. I have seen people cry and hug and laugh and scream, but in the end, they always get what they need and are the better for it.

The organized and tidy colour-coordinated binder served as a microcosm for how Karen and Levi worked together. Our discussions on each relevant topic were brief, formulated and driven by logic. Karen and Levi respected each other and worked well together. They let each other speak, shared a similar vision for the company and rarely found reason to disagree. I left the meeting surprised at how quickly we were able to organize the structure for their agreement and felt confident that their business would be a great success. I worked quickly to prepare a draft agreement for them, got minimal feedback and before you knew it, they had signed their shareholder agreement.

I figured this would be the last I would hear from Karen and Levi for a while, so I was surprised to receive a call from Levi only two months later. He sounded chipper and energetic, and as per usual he got straight to the point. "Hey Cory, long time no speak," he said. "Hi Levi," I replied cautiously, waiting to hear what was about to come my way. "Well, I just wanted to check in with you. We love the shareholder agreement and the business is doing really well. We were totally right about targeting the corporate market," he said. There was an awkward pause and I waited with bated breath. "Oh yeah, and great news! Karen is quitting the business. She wants to sell her shares to one of my best friends so we'll need your help with that." My jaw dropped and I had to quickly pick it up as we set a time to meet later in the week.

Upon greeting each other, we exchanged hugs once again and I was startled to see Karen beaming. "I'm so excited to be selling my shares," she screamed as we sat down to drink our green teas. "That is great," I said cautiously but encouragingly.

"Having done this work for the company with Levi, these past weeks, I've realized that this is exactly what I do NOT want to do." Karen paused as she looked at Levi and they both smiled. "So, I am going to sell my shares to Levi's friend Uriel. We are going to follow the shareholder agreement exactly to determine the fair price of the shares and guide us through the process of selling the shares." I looked at them for a moment and saw their big smiles shining deep into my eyes. It was a beautiful moment, because it helped me release judgement on something that we usually describe as "failure" or "quitting." The decision for Karen and Levi to stop working together was liberating – and it was great that they had put the structures in place *beforehand* to make this break-up all the easier. After the meeting, which was brief once again, I went back to my computer to effect the desired changes. It was all very simple, straightforward and easy.

I share this story because it provides a great illustration of a shareholder agreement working perfectly. It did not matter whether the company had lasted for years and grown tremendously wealthy or had never even got off the ground. The shareholder agreement was a very useful tool for two business owners to understand their rights and create an objective roadmap for dealing with certain situations. The majority of my work with shareholder agreements involves helping clients navigate through the challenges of not having a shareholder agreement, which is work that they happen to find very difficult, time consuming, very expensive and are often resentful about. I hope you learn from this story the benefits of communicating openly, organizing professionally and being proactive when interacting with the law. If nothing else, you will make a win-win situation of whatever circumstance life may throw your way.

Your Chapter Checklist

Here you go, the basics for choosing your business structure:

- You'll choose your business structure based on your exposure to liability, the need to protect your personal assets and the various tax factors in play with your business and earnings.
- Whichever structure you choose, be sure to finalize all steps required to properly complete the registration of that structure.
- Registering a company can create a separate legal entity, which protects your personal assets. A separate legal entity is not created for sole proprietorships and partnerships, meaning that your personal assets may be at risk within these structures.
- It is imperative to use Partnership Agreements and Shareholder Agreements.
- Have the difficult conversations before starting your business. This will help you in the long run.

Chapter 5

Waivers and Insurance Are Real Things

Intention

I am now going to discuss insurance and how it compliments your legal services, and then share very important information that you should know about waivers. Both of these areas fall under the "shield" aspect of the law, operating to help you protect your business, assets and reputation.

If you remember only two things from this chapter, remember the following points. On insurance, remember to *understand your policy.* Before you purchase insurance, get clear on everything you plan to do in your business, speak to your insurance broker/agent, find out your deductibles and make sure that your insurance will cover everything that you will be doing. On waivers, remember that waivers help you to communicate to people exactly what they will do while they are in your care, explain the risks and possible outcomes of participating in activities with you, and have them voluntarily agree to participate in the activities and release *you from any legal liability.*

What Is Insurance?

Here is the basic premise of how insurance operates: You continually pay little bits of money to an insurance company, and then if something wild and crazy happens the insurance company will cover the big bill for you. Insurance is a massive industry. There are many different types of insurance – pet insurance, car insurance, life insurance, home insurance, travel insurance. The list goes on and on. They all operate in the same way. Basically, the insurance policy provides you with coverage for a massive range of things that could happen, and if one of those things actually happens then the insurance company will cover what you owe – the amount of which would be much higher than the cost of your insurance policy.

Just like I'm not an accountant, I'm not an insurance broker either. I am going to provide a general overview of how insurance affects yoga professionals, and I will strive to make the information as practical as possible. Just to be clear, I am only going to deal with professional liability insurance, which is the insurance that protects you in the course of operating your business. Even in the field of professional liability insurance, there are many different specialized insurance services for doctors, lawyers, architects, engineers and – yes, yogis. When we discuss insurance in this chapter, we are doing so only in the context of professional liability insurance for health professionals, specifically yoga practitioners and business operators.

Practical Tips on Insurance

Understand Your Policy. This means understanding the details of your relationship with your insurance company, specifically how much they will cover you for; how much you will have to pay out of pocket to use your policy (in other words, the amount of your "deductible"); and in what instances you will or will not be covered. This last point is the most important, because if you are paying for insurance, you will want to make sure that your policy covers you for the things you will actually do. The worst-case scenario is when you operate your business under the impression that you are covered, only to find out that you are not covered and have to pay out of pocket to resolve an issue that insurance would normally cover.

When Am I Covered? This is so important that it bears repeating. One of the biggest challenges for my yogi clients is getting clear on what their insurance policy covers them for. There is a very easy solution: You can call up your insurance broker (the person who manages your relationship with an insurance company) and ask them about the specifics of your policy. If the company you have chosen to work with has any form of decent customer service, they will happily chat with you on the phone and walk you through the details of your policy. The key to preparing for this conversation is getting clear on exactly what you do in your business, where you do it and who is doing it for you.

Get Staff to Have Their Own Insurance. It has become almost standard procedure for yoga and fitness studios to require teachers to have their own insurance (with minimum liabilities varying, usually starting at $1 million). This is a really great practice to follow because it helps prevent a lot of problems from developing. And in the event of an issue, it will ensure that there is at least some kitty of cash to resolve the problem. Keep in mind that most *legal issues revolve around money*. Insurance makes sure that at least some money is available to resolve the situation. The alternative, a lack of money, creates great stress and big problems, leading to sleepless nights and possibly the forfeiture of personal assets. Long story short – get insurance.

Hound Your Insurance Broker until You Get It. One practical tip that I always share at workshops is the importance of asking an insurance broker or agent every question under the sun about an insurance plan. *Remember*, sometimes people care about you more when they want your business and less when they have your business. So, the clearer you are on what you need for coverage the better – and do not be afraid to ask about all the scenarios in which you may or may not be covered. The time to ask is before you make the purchase. Lots of insurance agents are lovely and provide excellent customer service, but you will definitely have their attention when they feel close to securing you as a client.

Waivers ARE a Thing

I am not sure who has been spreading nasty rumours about waivers, but whoever it is should probably stop. There is gossip going around that waivers are not really a thing, that they are not enforceable and do not do anything. In a sentence: NOT TRUE.

A waiver is a document that you can use to protect yourself from legal liability when you are taking care of other people. When I say "taking care of other people," just think of any scenario in which you are responsible for another person. At law you may be said to have a "duty of care" towards that person. This basically means that the law implies a relationship in which you have a duty to take care of the other person by ensuring they will be safe in your care. So for example, you can have a duty of care towards others in the following scenarios:

- You are teaching another person yoga.
- You are hosting a yoga event or retreat in which another person participates.
- A person walks into your yoga studio to participate in a class.

- You are paying someone to teach a class in your yoga studio.

When you have someone sign a waiver, they release you from liability that arises from your obligation to ensure they stay safe. They give up their rights to bring a legal action against you for certain things that happen while they are in your care. So, in super plain English: Waivers are documents in which people agree not to hold you responsible for what happens to them while they are in your care.

In practice, waivers *are* a real thing. I want to avoid making this book too legal-y, so I will not discuss any cases or things like that. But you can look up how the Supreme Courts of Canada and the United States have ruled many times on the enforceability of waivers (look it up, yo!). Most of the time, people fight in court to try to stop waivers from applying. Lawyers will get super creative in explaining why a waiver should not apply. There are books written on this topic alone. But for our purposes, please know that *waivers do work when they are properly drafted*. They are by no means a panacea, but they are a very important foundational piece in protecting your business.

The law allows people to agree to anything – and be bound to that agreement – so long as the agreement is not illegal or inherently unfair (i.e. one person abusing power or influence over another). As such, when it comes to waivers, the courts are generally cool with letting people sign away their legal rights, so long as those people are *properly and clearly informed* about the sort of situation they are getting themselves into. The law does not interfere with people agreeing on certain things, but the law will demand that the agreements clearly communicate the appropriate content.

A waiver can do more than just limit your liability should

something go terribly wrong while you are responsible for the well-being of another person. A waiver is also a great way to communicate with people exactly what they should expect when working with you. I love how a waiver is really the first touch point (literally) for your clients to interact with your brand, and how as such, it should be friendly, welcoming and loving – assuming that this is the vibe you are trying to create. You can have the document set the tone for the energy that you are inviting into your business.

What Needs to Be in Every Waiver

There are a few simple elements that should be present in all waivers. Before we get to them, this is a great opportunity to remind you of the importance of open and honest communication. In a pragmatic sense, a waiver is an opportunity for you to fairly communicate to your students exactly what they will be doing while spending time with you and the risks that can arise from those activities.

A few examples of what I mean:

- If you want students to do partner work in your yoga class, have you explained this to the students and informed them that injuries can happen when they work with other students?
- If you are taking students on a retreat to a foreign country, have you explained who will be responsible for their well-being during the free time away from class? Is it your responsibility if a student gets into trouble or falls ill while abroad? (Yes, one of my clients had a student who was arrested during a retreat in Thailand.)
- If you are teaching a student who has a pre-existing injury or is not medically fit to practice, have you

communicated that they must tell you about their condition before they start the class?

- If you are teaching a pre-natal yoga class, have you communicated the wholly different risks that arise in these classes as compared with normal yoga?

Now, I know what you *might* be doing at this moment. You might be thinking two things: 1) This guy is such a stickler; and 2) these things never happen. Anyone who knows me will tell you that I am not detail oriented. I'm a pretty laid-back guy and don't get too worked up about specifics. I have included these examples because the lawyer side of me has seen all of them happen. I am not trying to scare you, I am just trying to help you.

Getting to *the juice*, here are things that every waiver needs to do:

1. State that unless the waiver is signed, the participant may not join class;
2. Let people know exactly what you will be doing with them;
3. Let them know the risks of doing these activities with you;
4. Let them know what injuries/problems can happen if the aforementioned risks materialize;
5. Give them an opportunity to acknowledge the risks and the injuries/problems that can happen as a result of the risks, and then let them voluntarily choose to participate in the activities; and
6. Indicate that by voluntarily participating in the activities while being fully informed of those activities and risks, they agree not to hold you legally responsible for anything that happens to them and they release you from all liability.

Waiver FAQ

Here are answers to some questions that I always hear when it comes to waivers:

Question 1: What Are the Most Common Mistakes That People Make with Waivers?

Answer: The first common mistake that I see in waivers is that they are not specific enough in describing what activities are covered. A waiver will not be effective if it does not really describe for your students the activities they will be doing and the risks of doing those activities. Of course, everything will depend on the students *voluntarily participating* in the activities while being aware of the risks and possible outcomes. But their voluntary agreement will be nullified if you are not clear enough about what activities you will be doing together, or if you tell them that you will be doing one thing and then do another. People cannot consent to a waiver of liability for certain activities if they do not know what activities they will be doing.

The second most common mistake I see is that waivers are a bit vague about the injuries or damages that a person may suffer. For example, I see a lot of waivers that mention possible injuries by listing things like "get hurt'" or "suffer pain," which are not really specific enough. Courts and judges will not accept legal terms that are not sufficiently clear. So it is important to be descriptive and honest about what can actually happen. The best way to tackle this is to imagine that something goes wrong in your class, and then read the waiver to see if a reasonable person would have been adequately warned about what happened in your hypothetical scenario.

This will be a good indication of how healthy your waiver is.

Question 2: Do Waivers Work Online?

Answer: Yes. The nature of operating a business and working with customers has evolved with technology. Online waivers are accepted as waivers, but there are a few things to keep in mind. The big thing with waivers is that people can only agree to release you from liability if they know what activities they will be doing with you and what risks arise out of those activities. Here is the problem when we do this online: *How do we know that people have read the waiver?* We don't. And that is why we have to take great lengths to show that we did everything we could to encourage people to read the waiver. Sure, they have to click "I agree to be bound to the terms and conditions of this waiver," but it is possible they will do so without ever reading anything.

So, we have to take responsibility for our tribe and be extra careful to encourage them to read the waiver. One way to do this is by only letting them click "agree" after they have scrolled through the whole agreement. You might have seen other online businesses do this when they update their terms. The point of doing it is that you can show you were reasonable. If something happens and a person does not want their waiver to hold up, they would say, "Well, it was online and I just clicked without reading." In this scenario, your response would be, "We forced you to go through the whole agreement before you could agree to it and you agreed that you had read the terms." Now who seems to be acting more reasonably? Online waivers are a thing, and taking steps to show that they are as reasonable as possible is the best way to protect yourself while operating online.

Question 3: Do Waivers Need a Witness?

Answer: There are some legal documents for which you need a witness present (for example, the proper writing and signing of a will), but a waiver of liability is not one of them. The main thing to remember when you have people sign a waiver or any other legal agreement is that they must have "capacity." This means that they must fully understand the agreement and have the capacity to enter into it, understanding its consequences. If someone is not old enough, they will not have capacity to enter into an agreement, and thus you cannot enforce the terms of the agreement upon them. In this case, it is helpful to put something in the agreement saying that if someone is under the age of majority (depending on the rules of your jurisdiction), they cannot agree to the terms and must have their legal guardian or parent agree to be bound to those terms on their behalf.

Question 4: Should I Include the Word Death in My Waiver?

Answer: Tough one. This always comes up with my clients and I would say that they have been split down the middle. Some have no problem using the word death and others are very uncomfortable using it. This makes sense, I suppose, as death can be a very uncomfortable thing. I am currently drafting a waiver for kids' yoga and discussing with my client whether or not to include the word here. Generally speaking, my personal position is to include it. The truth is, people can die anywhere and things usually get *highly litigious* when someone dies, because everyone is super emotional and the estate wants to get as much money as possible to compensate for the loss of life.

People have heart attacks anywhere and everywhere. Death is part of life, and while it is a bummer to remind people of that when they are going on a retreat or coming to your yoga class, you do need to protect yourself adequately. I do, however, understand both sides and support the decision either way.

Question 5: Should I Ask People to List Previous Injuries or Medical Conditions?

Answer: This is another question that depends totally on personal preference. Asking about injuries or medical conditions is only beneficial if you actually use the information instead of just filing it away. A lot of clients ask me, "If I learn that someone has an injury, am I then responsible for treating it? Do I owe a higher duty of care to the client once I know about their injury?" This too is a tough question. Yes, legally, if you ask about previous medical conditions or injuries and learn that your client has them, your responsibility to ensure their safety may be heightened. But the alternative is that you do not ask, and depending on the circumstances, this could be deemed negligent. Is offering a yoga class and not asking about medical conditions or injuries responsible? Only you can decide that. Again, as I have mentioned throughout this book, I encourage you to draft and use agreements that you are comfortable with.

Question 6: Should I Include Something about Adjustments?

Answer: Adjustments are a legal issue because they deal with consent to being touched. This is a very serious deal and something that studios should address with great intention and compassion. We have seen issues arise in the past when some instructors have inappropriately touched students, which is abhorrent behaviour that has no place in society, anywhere.

Should consent to touching be included in a waiver? There are a couple of considerations here. Firstly, a person may change their mind about wanting adjustments from one day to the next, or depending on the instructor, so it may not help to have the information on a piece of paper they signed one day. We are always changing. Secondly, a lot of this comes down to how you use the information you collect. If you ask people whether they want to be adjusted and then file the answers away in your office without communicating them to your teachers, it could happen that a student who did not consent to being touched gets an adjustment in class. That would be a big problem. Thirdly, including adjustments in a waiver can be a useful practice if you are using the document to ensure the client's comfort and explain the intention behind adjustments. Some students find it intimidating to raise their hand in class and would prefer the anonymity of sharing their preference in a document. As well, some students only want soft adjustments and do not feel comfortable pushing their bodies.

Please know that it is totally your choice when it comes to deciding how to address the issue of adjustments in class. In my opinion, no yoga teacher should touch a student without receiving permission first. End of story. You may have a different perspective, which you are most entitled to. *I firmly encourage you to obtain permission* from people before you touch students or offer adjustments, and that you also explain why you are making such adjustments. There are lots of clever ways that the industry is dealing with adjustments, such as placing adjustment cards beside mats to let students choose if they want adjustments during that particular class. You can find many ways to creatively deal with adjustments. You may decide to include this in your agreements or not.

Story: The Class That Started Yoga Law

It was a night that would change my life forever. But as the evening was unfolding, it felt more like a comedy of miscommunications and errors that would lead to absolutely nothing. This is, I presume, how most remarkable adventures begin.

On a dark and rainy Friday in November, I was sitting on the 18th floor of the PwC building on Howe Street in my little cubicle at Dentons, the largest law firm in the world. I had spent the majority of the week in that cubicle working as an articling student. For those who don't know (I didn't before law school), articling is a fancy term used to denote a year-long internship in which a person magically transforms from a feeble law student into a high-powered lawyer – right before your eyes! Think purgatory but with a suit, tie and decent coffee.

My week had been especially difficult. I was working on a challenging assignment with one of the firm's top partners, and I had put in my time in the form of early mornings, late evenings and off-the-clock stress – a specialty of big law firms. I was planning to spend the weekend with my work until I received a message from a dear friend named Sue at around 2 p.m. "Hey Cory – hope your week has been going well! Alex is doing a special pop-up yoga class tonight at 7 and Pam and I want you to join. Location is 285 9th St. We haven't seen you in a while and want to practice together. We can cook vegan food afterwards. Let me know. Be love!"

The moment I finished reading the message I was committed to going to the class. It had been a strenuous week without enough "me time" and yoga with Alex was always the fix. I glanced up at my screen and scanned over the document that had taken up my entire week. "No one is even going to read this," I thought to myself as I looked over all my research. I closed my eyes and took a few breaths, calculating exactly what I would need to do to get out on time. "I can do this," I said to myself, then put my head down and got busy. The next thing I knew, I looked up and it was 18:43. I scrambled to organize my things, knowing that I would have to return to my desk on the weekend, and booked it outside to my bicycle. I strapped on my helmet convinced that I would make it to class.

My heart got a little bit warmer as I pressed the button to call Sue. Sue and Pam were two girls I had met at Alex's yoga class and were in the midst of their undergraduate degrees at Simon Fraser University. There were pure yogis in the sense that they lived love, all the time. The girls could only be found together and were always cooking some healthy and delicious vegan food or talking about yoga. They both lived with permanent smiles. It had taken only about six months of seeing each other at Alex's weekly yoga classes to plan a hang outside of the studio, and once we did we realized we would be great friends. From that point on, we often went to yoga or cooked or hung out at the beach.

Sue and Pam were a very welcome addition to my life now that I had started articles and begun to show the first signs of the "M" word – *maturity*. I had been travelling the world since age nineteen and my current gig at Dentons was the first time I had looked in the mirror every morning and asked, "Is this it? Ten vacation days a year?" I had seemingly transformed from a traveller to a corporate lawyer overnight, not feeling the change within myself but seeing it all around me. The joys of being with Sue and Pam arose mostly from their company but also from the freedom and ease their lives represented. I loved those girls and always will.

Sue had told me the location of the class but forgot to mention whether the class was on the east or west side of the street. I had about three minutes to spare and decided to go east. My heart was racing when I arrived at 285 East 9th Street only to find an abandoned industrial building. I knocked on the door and peeked inside, but the interior was filled with scrap metals and looked like a disorganized construction site. Clearly this was not the studio. I glanced at my phone and saw it was 19:04. I lowered my head with a feeling of defeat and let go of making it to class.

I began dialling the girls but I knew that class had started and the chances of them picking up were slim. I tried Sue. No luck. I tried Pam. No Luck. I was so dejected that I began walking with my bike towards home. This is when you know that a cyclist is upset; you see them walking with a perfectly good bike, oblivious that they should be riding it. I really needed this class – not just to de-stress from the week, but also because I always connected deeply with Alex's teachings. When she spoke in class everything just made sense. Whenever I read Krishnamurti or Osho or Watts or de Botton, I found myself underlining every sentence. And when Alex shared her gifts in class, I found myself mentally underlining every word that left her mouth. I lamented letting the evening slip through my fingers.

Then out of nowhere, I felt a vibration in my pocket and heard my phone begin to ring. I clicked my earphones immediately and heard a high-pitched loving scream: "Ah Coryyyy, where are you… hahaha." It was Pam. A huge smile found its way to my face. "We are waiting for you. Everyone is late, we aren't starting for ten minutes. You have to come," she said insistently. I was elated. I confirmed the correct address and was surprised to hear that class was taking place in a location that used to be a clothing store but was under renovations. I did not ask any questions and just rode to my destination. The day was saved: I would make Alex's class.

The scene inside the class was unique. Alex had a very big following in Vancouver simply because she was an exceptional teacher. Going to one of her classes always felt like going home. It was a combination of the familiar faces, the familiar smell of incense and the familiar music I knew I would hear at her class. Despite all the markings of familiarity, this class felt different. Way different. There were some mats strewn across the floor in a disorganized fashion. Three giant pillars jutted out of different sections of the room, creating barriers and obstacles for a clean space to practice. It was very clear this space was not intended to be used for a yoga class.

I was not really concerned with the layout of the space, especially once I found Sue and Pam. Somehow, I made eye contact with both of them at the same time – this is how everything seemed to go with the girls – always together. We enjoyed a massive hug that turned into a little jumping circle. The girls really did live love. We began catching up until we heard Alex's voice. "Hi everyone, welcome to class. As you can see, we aren't in our normal space, but a friend offered this space to do class and I thought it would be a fun space to enjoy together. We are asking for a $20 donation from anyone who would like to practice. After you've paid, please find your way to your mat and we will prepare to begin class." We shared our final hugs, with the energy in the room clearly changing from excitement to focus.

As I walked over to Alex to give my donation, I could not help thinking that the venue was a poor choice for a yoga class.

I kept my thoughts to myself and simply dropped my money in the bin and smiled at Alex. As I made my way back to my mat, and then sat on my block and breathed before class, I randomly thought about how I did not have to sign a waiver to practice that evening. Studios normally made students sign a waiver before their first time practicing in a space or with a certain studio company, but this time nothing needed to be signed. I felt my stomach turn.

As these facts dawned on me, I suddenly started looking at the "studio" through a lawyer's lens. A lawyer's lens is a unique way of looking at things and not one that I love to employ, but certainly one I do appreciate. Basically, when you are a lawyer, you have to anticipate that the outcome of every situation or relationship will end as horribly as it possibly can. Literally, you think to yourself, "What is the worst possible outcome that can arise from this activity?" and use that as the starting point for writing up an agreement. Law school provides excellent training for this, as students read cases upon cases about the least likely scenarios that somehow materialize, ultimately proving the point that you should prepare and protect your clients for the worst.

I peered around the room and suddenly grew quite concerned. There were so many hazards and dangers in the room but no one had signed any documents. I began my breathing meditation – four breaths in, six breaths out – and told myself to be a yogi and not a lawyer. Everything would be just fine, all I had to do was focus on my brain and enjoy the practice. I concluded that I would speak to Alex after class and offer to help her with her waivers before the next class.

Class began normally with some chanting and sun salutations, and soon I forgot entirely about the risks around the room. It did not take me long to remember all the reasons why I loved Alex's classes. She had a very fluid and comfortable way of leading students through the physical practice, and without doubt she was exceptionally talented at explaining complex yogic principles in a very simple and digestible way. Her classes were filled with entertaining stories from various lineages and illustrated principles that I could connect with in my everyday life. After most classes, I would approach Alex and ask her questions about my own personal experiences or doubts. Time after time, Alex would deliver helpful guidance in the form of an excellent author I had never read or a band that I had never listened to. Alex was the first teacher who really helped me bring "depth" to my yoga practice, and there was nothing that I enjoyed more than being in her classes.

I was feeling perfect in my body and in my breath as we approached the end of our warm-ups. This was the reason I had rushed from the office – this escape, this connection. Then suddenly I was startled by a jostling noise right by the door at the back of the room. The noise was followed by a few whispers and the sound of mats being moved in the back row. Clearly, someone had arrived late and was trying to join practice. "Please make space for the people who have just joined and welcome them as you would want to be welcomed," Alex said as all of the students peered to the back to see what the fuss was about. "Okay," she said, "back to work now," and the class resumed as if nothing had happened.

As I turned forward and brought my attention back to my mat, I could not help but see that one of the girls who had just entered the space had placed her mat right beside a giant pillar. I was well on my way to feeling blissed out from class, so I did not think too much about it except that it seemed weird she would practice yoga in such an uncomfortable space. It was not until we got to the arm balance part of class that things took a turn for the worse. This was the part of class when the very talented and experienced students popped up into impressive upside-down positions while I chilled out in shoulder stand waiting for them to finish.

As I leaned back on my shoulders and lifted my legs, I heard a loud thump and a shrill cry from the back row. I did not see what happened but noticed a crowd suddenly surround the girl who was practicing beside the pillar. She was on the floor, writhing in pain and grasping her right arm. She lay there for a moment and then was helped up and guided outside of the room. Everyone was shocked. I caught a glance of Pam and Sue – again mysteriously at the exact same time – and they looked very concerned. Alex tried to play it off very casually, telling the class that everything was alright and asking us to return to our poses. It was not clear what had happened or how it had happened, but it was clear that someone had been hurt.

I was still very much in bliss mode and did not come to process what had happened until the class began an extended savasana. I reconnected with my breath and slowly began to put all of the pieces together in my mind: We were practicing outside the classroom, in a space that was unfit for practice, without anyone signing a waiver of liabilities. This was trouble.

My body began to twitch slightly as I reviewed the situation through my lawyer's lens. I thought about the student being seriously injured – like not being able to work for a few months and needing to come after Alex to be compensated for the lost time at work. Even worse, I envisioned a situation in which the student suffered an injury that resulted in long-term disability and Alex was responsible to pay exorbitant damages. I thought for a moment about Alex's three young kids and her family. Although she was an amazing yoga teacher, she was not very rich. Whether she knew it or not, her livelihood was at stake.

I decided in that moment that I would find a way to help Alex, to draft some agreements that would make sure she would be okay. I was certain that I could draft documents that Alex could understand and be proud of using. What an idea, I thought – doing law for yogis.

It took everything inside me not to jump up and share all of this information with Alex as we neared the final moments of our meditation. I patiently waited for our final chant of *aum* before opening my eyes. I felt as if I had taken a crazy trip through my mind, seeing the risks of the situation all around me. However, once I sat up and plopped myself down onto my block, I surveyed the room to find that everything looked completely normal. It was clear that I was the only person who had considered the gravity of the situation and that the rest of the group was completely oblivious to what had happened – and what could have happened! Later, when I eventually spoke to Alex, I saw that she, too, was oblivious to the risks of her practice.

I waited for the usual crowd around Alex to disperse before I approached my favourite teacher. There was so much to share and I wanted to scream it all aloud. "Alex," I said with a big exhale and a concerned but loving look. "Cory," she said in reply. Then there was a silence; I had so much to say that I was almost unable to say anything. "Yes…" she said, edging me along and encouraging me to spit it out. I began fumbling. I did not know how to say all of the things that I felt without perhaps coming across as rude or ungrateful or nosy. Telling someone else what to do is never fun.

"Alex, I don't know how to say this, so I am just going to say it," I said, "but please know that it is only coming from a place of love." Alex looked on, keeping eye contact but growing seemingly disinterested. I took a deep breath and kept going.

"What happened tonight was unprofessional and I don't mean the class itself or your practice, but just the fact that you had class in an unsafe space, no one signed waivers and someone actually got hurt." Alex looked at me for a few moments. "Okay," she said. "Ummm... maybe." And that was it. I was about to launch into my premeditated diatribe but instead just let it go. "Well, I enjoyed class as usual, so thanks for that," I said with a forced smile. I slowly took my cue to leave as another student came to talk to Alex.

My heart dropped for a second as I walked away. Alex really did not get it. She really did not understand the risks of what could have happened. It was at that moment I realized that I could not blame or fault her at all. Alex was an incredible yoga teacher and a proven professional at leading classes, developing a following and sharing her beautiful gifts with her community, but she was ignorant about the law. As I delved deeper into this thought, it did not take me long to realize that if I had not gone to law school, I would have been ignorant about the law, too. For a moment, I pictured an alternative life that I could have lived without law school – without learning about the concepts of trial advocacy, duty of care and non-insane automatism. The simplicity of it made so much sense. In my mind I concluded: "Of course she does not know about this, she did not go to law school."

As I stumbled to the door, still stuck in my daze, I saw two sets of eyes jump up in front of me. "Corrrrryyyyy," said Sue and Pam as they both jumped out to hug me at the same time. "We love youuuuuu," they said before I could wrap my arms around them. We had a big group hug and the girls laid out the specifics for the meal we were going to make – a combination of veggies from the farmer's market, homemadehummus and brown rice with lentils. A vegan dream! We cycled together to their home, talking and laughing about how much we loved class and all the wonderful things that friends can find reasons to laugh about.

When we arrived, I began cutting vegetables and remembered the incident in Alex's class. "Didn't you girls think that the setup for class was sketchy?" I said, intentionally avoiding the subject of waivers. "That was sorta dangerous," said one. "Yeah, totally unsafe, I couldn't believe it," said the other in a reassuring tone. I continued: "I spoke to Alex afterwards because I'm sort of worried for her, but she didn't seem to be bothered by it. She's got her young kids and if something went wrong, she would really be putting her family at risk." The girls thought for a second. They each took a bite of carrot simultaneously and then gave a concerned, slightly scared nod at the same time. There was silence until I heard the sound of another carrot crunch. It was clear that we had stumbled onto a real problem here.

Over the next few days I did not have too much time to dwell on the legal challenges of yogis, as I was pretty swamped finishing up my major project at work. I had told a few of my co-workers the story, but I got little traction or attention. My cry to help yogis was met with deaf ears and blank stares. "Yoga, yeah, my wife tells me that I should really do that but I can't even touch my toes," was a typical response. It was clear that my co-workers were not listening to me. This conversation was not meant for downtown.

I decided to start having conversations with people who would be interested. I began going to my favourite yoga teachers and asking them general questions to see what they knew about liability, waivers and the like. Two things became clear fairly quickly – they did not know about general legal principles and they were not interested to find out. They were mainly concerned with – surprise, surprise – yoga! This discovery was equally encouraging and daunting. With each new conversation, it became increasingly obvious that there was a real need for yoga professionals to learn about their legal responsibilities and rights. I realized that the big challenge would be communicating my message to this community. How could I possibly transform an industry that favours karma over contracts and poses over professionalism? I knew that no matter what happened, this was going to be fun.

In order to tie up the loose ends, it is worth noting that I did a bit of detective work and discovered that the girl who got injured in Alex's class suffered a shattered wrist. I never contacted her and did not speak to Alex about the issue ever again.

In hindsight, it all makes perfect sense how it happened: The wrong address, almost bailing on class, showing up late and sticking around to be exposed to a very important lesson. Life works in this way. The most fascinating and interesting experiences reveal themselves in the least predictable ways. This is what makes every moment and every day so exciting.

Takeaway: The key thing to understand is that a waiver must honestly tell people what you will be doing with them and what they can expect, and then let them decide on their own whether they want to waive their legal rights.

Alex's story highlights the risks of operating without a waiver, but also the importance of having the waiver communicate exactly what you will be doing with your students and where you will be doing it. Even if Alex had used her normal studio waiver, it may not have covered her liability because it would have contemplated yoga classes in a safe and controlled environment. In reality, the pop-up class was in a space that was unsuitable for safe yoga practice. When we all arrived for the class, we reasonably assumed that we would be practicing in a safe place. Why would our teacher put us in any other situation, right? So, if there had been a waiver (which there was not), we probably would have waived our legal rights with respect to a yoga class in a safe space. BUT would we have agreed to waive our rights if we had known the class would be in an unprofessional and unsafe environment, with dangerous obstacles strewn across the room? I am not sure, but at least we would have been *informed about the risks* so that we could each make our own individual decision.

Your Chapter Checklist

Waivers and insurance, super simplified:
- Make sure you understand your insurance policy and feel free to speak with your insurance broker/agent until you are super clear on what you covered for and what you are not covered for.
- Waivers are a real thing and will stand to protect you in a court of law.
- Waivers must be written clearly and specifically, applying to the services and activities you will be doing with your students.

Chapter 6

The Difference between Independent Contractors + Employees

Please Note: Specifically in the United States of America, the current legal trend is for yoga studios to classify their teachers as employees and not as contractors. While this is a more expensive set up, governments have been cracking down on the employee/contractor distinction, in favour of seeing yoga teachers at studios as employees. The information in this chapter shares general legal principles, but we highly encourage you to speak with a lawyer in your jurisdiction before deciding how you will classify those who teach at your studio.

Intention

Most people in the yoga community, like most other people, do not really understand the difference between an independent contractor ("IC") and an employee, or why the difference matters. In this chapter I am going to explain the difference and tell you definitively why it does matter. If you operate or work for a yoga studio, you are directly affected by this area of law. The good news is that I promised you FUN, so I am committed to explaining this subject as simply and entertainingly as possible. Sit back, enjoy the stories and keep an open mind about how the system operates in order to understand where you fit in.

If you remember only one thing from this chapter, remember that the more control you have over someone working for you, the more likely it is that they are your employee and not a contractor. An employee is someone who works for your business, whereas a contractor is someone who runs their own business and simply carries out a service for yours. Employees have protection at law from employment standards legislation, whereas contractors do not have specific legislation outlining their relationship with you. You can get serious penalties for misclassifying an employee as a contractor.

The First Thing You Need to Know

The starting point for any discussion of the IC/employee distinction is that a person is not a "contractor" or an "employee" just because you call them that. Instead, the nature of the working relationship will determine whether or not someone is a contractor or an employee. And the main feature of the relationship that will determine this is how much control one party has over the other. The more control that you have over a person who works for you, the more likely it is that the person is your employee. The less control, the more likely it is that person is a contractor.

I was recently talking to some new clients about how they were building their team of staff. "We're going to have a few contractors and a few employees," they said. My ears perked up. "Hmm..." I responded. "How will you decide which are which?" I asked. One of my clients responded proudly, "Some of them will feel more like employees and some will feel more like contractors." I loved this response, I really did. And I wished that the law could operate so that certain rules would apply depending on whether we felt like it or not. But I knew that unfortunately this is not how it always works. When I responded, I tried not to crush my clients' goal of building a dream team, and I informed them that the *determining factor* would be the type of work their staff performs and the way the roles are organized.

As you move forward, just remember that a person is not inherently a contractor or employee. Their classification will depend on the relationship they have with the person who pays them, especially the type of work they do and the way they do that work. It does not really matter if you hire someone and call the working arrangement an "Independent Contractor Agreement," because at law the person may be an employee due to the nature of the work they do for you and the amount of control you exercise over them as they do that work.

The Big Picture Perspective

What are independent contractors? They are people you hire who run their own business, usually outside the scope of what you do professionally. You have very little control over how they do their job and you support them minimally in the performance of their work. For example: My amazing friend Christie Baumgartner runs the coolest yoga retreats in British Columbia and across the world. She works with a graphic designer to come up with beautiful posters advertising the exotic locations and dreamy experiences that she facilitates. The graphic designer is clearly a contractor because they use their own materials, offer their services wherever and whenever they want, and are not controlled by Christie in how they do their work.

What is an employee? This is a person who works as a staff member for a business. For example, the administrative staff at a yoga studio may have a set schedule (Monday–Friday, 9–5), work from a specific location (the studio), use the studio's equipment (studio computers), do their jobs according to the studio's specific instructions (studio control) and have no financial incentive based on performance. Clearly, they are under the control of the yoga studio in every aspect of how they do their job and do not operate their own business. As such, they are unquestionably employees.

Who decides and why do they care? The government decides whether a worker is an employee or a contractor. Firstly, the government wants to ensure that it gets paid all of its taxes, since contractors are responsible for paying their own taxes whereas employers deduct tax payments from their employees' paycheques. Secondly, the government wants to protect the rights of workers and ensure that they are treated fairly, because employees are entitled to significantly more protections than contractors under employment laws and standards (i.e. overtime, vacation pay, notice for firing, pension contributions, etc.).

How is the decision made? The government will make its decision based on the scope and nature of a worker's services, looking at the whole relationship and not just the parties' arrangement (i.e. the employment agreement or IC agreement). More specifically, the government will apply a "control test." This means that it will look at how much control the worker is under in different areas of the working relationship, weigh these factors against each other and then – voila – decide if the worker is a contractor or employee. I want to keep you awake so I will only list a few of the things that the government will consider when applying the control test, just to give you an idea:

- Does the worker decide their own schedule?
- Does the worker use their own equipment?
- Is the worker allowed to work for anyone else in the same capacity?
- Are the wages incentivized by performance (i.e. does the worker get paid more if they sign up more clients)?
- Does the worker have to perform their services from a specific location, or can they work from wherever they want?

Practically Speaking, Why Does It Matter?

When a worker provides services to another person for money, both parties enter into a relationship at law. What they owe to each other and what they are responsible for will vary depending on the *type* of relationship. If the worker is a contractor, they must behave in a certain way. However, if the worker is an employee, the employer (i.e. the person who pays them) must behave in a certain way. It is cheaper to hire a contractor and that is why some businesses try to do so. However, small business owners are at risk of getting fines plus interest for incorrectly classifying employees as contractors. Recently, governments across North America have been making it more difficult for businesses to hire contractors, favouring the employee relationship. This is a constantly changing area of law which needs your attention.

Here are some basic principles that will help us understand the difference in legal status between independent contractors and employees:

- Independent contractors are responsible for paying their own taxes.
- Employers are responsible for deducting employees' taxes from their paycheques, in addition to other

types of benefits (i.e. employment insurance, pension contributions, etc.).

- Employees enjoy protections under the law regarding their basic rights, including how much they can receive as minimum pay, how they can be fired and whether they are entitled to any vacation days.
- Employers will generally be held legally responsible for the actions of their employees, but not the actions of independent contractors (subject to specific circumstances).
- Independent contractors are allowed to keep the copyright and other intellectual property (IP) rights to things they create for someone who hires them unless the parties agree otherwise.
- By contrast, employers keep the IP rights in things that employees make, as long as they are made in the course of the employees' employment (subject to specific circumstances).

And here are some classic issues that arise around the IC/employee distinction to help us understand why the distinction matters so much:

- A contractor does not pay their taxes, gets audited and then claims that they are an employee. The government catches a sniff and audits the studio.
- A company treats its employees like contractors, depriving them of their legal rights as employees.
- A client gets hurt and then blames the teacher (supposedly a contractor), who then argues that they are an employee and that the company should be held responsible.
- A teacher creates a new class or teacher manual for a studio, believing that they have kept the IP rights as a

contractor and can sell their creation to other companies. However, the studio forbids the sale claiming that it owns the ideas in the creation because the teacher is an employee.

Four Issues to Consider

Issue 1: Do the Right Thing

There should be no judgement value associated with classifying a worker as a contractor or an employee. Contractors are not better than employees or vice versa. There seems to be a general conception that having contractors is easier than having employees, but this is not always the case. It is simply cheaper. When you work with a contractor, you will have to worry about whether they pay their taxes and the fact that they own the IP in work they create (unless agreed otherwise). You will also have less control over a contractor than an employee.

The truth is, it should not matter which category of worker is better. All that should matter is the type of work they do for you and how they do it, because that is what will determine what category they fall under. Do the right thing. If you are going to treat contractors like employees, do the right thing and hire them as employees so they get the proper protections and workers' rights they deserve. If you value your people and act with integrity, you owe them what they fairly deserve. Society has made rules for us to follow, and that is the point of all of this. Do the right thing.

Issue 2: Government + Taxes

The sooner you realize that the government cares about whether you are an IC or an employee, the quicker you will begin to clean up your act. This area of law is predominantly about money, specifically taxes, and you do not need me to tell you that when something is about money, specifically taxes, people CARE. The government, both provincial/state and federal, is interested in collecting all of its taxes. That is the reason why this really matters. There are a bunch of secondary and tertiary reasons, which are about how the classification will affect you, but for the most part this is about money. It is not even about your money; it is about the government's money.

Now, if you do not pay your taxes and upset the government, they may open an AUDIT against you. Similarly, if you operate a business that employs employees but calls them contractors, the government may open an AUDIT against you. Being audited = no bueno. Really no bueno. Audits are an outcome that we seek to avoid at all costs. They are not fun, expensive and they are stressful, so let's do everything we can to play by the rules and avoid this happening.

Issue 3: Ownership of IP

This is a MAJOR issue to be aware of when working with contractors, and one that I constantly come across in my work. Please just understand this: You own the IP in something that an employee creates for your business (as long as making it was in their normal course of employment), whereas contractors will often have rights and entitlements to any IP that they create for you *unless agreed otherwise*. That means that unless you come to an agreement that you will own the IP in what your contractor makes for you, it is possible that although you can use what they make, you may not own it – and that could prevent you from licensing it or earning as much profit from it as you might like.

A classic example of this issue arises when you work with photographers and videographers, who retain the rights to anything they create for you. Before you build your logo, or promote a video of your studio or retreats, make sure that you can keep the IP or at least do whatever you want with it in the future. I have included a story in the next chapter that has EVERYTHING to do with this issue, illustrating how it can come up when working with contractors and organizing yoga teacher trainings ("Story: Copyright Issue"). Feel free to skip ahead and have a read of it now.

Issue 4: Treating Contractors like Employees without Offering the Benefits of Employment

Being ingrained in the yoga community, I have a lot of friends who are professional yoga teachers. They are remarkable heroes who have decided to commit their lives to teaching yoga full time, which is no easy task. Depending on the market in which they provide their classes, they can be taken advantage of by big studios that seemingly have a monopoly in the market. Sometimes, the studios will take advantage of their size or the market to create relationships with yoga teachers that are neither legal nor fair. More often than not, they will hire teachers as contractors and try to enjoy the benefits of treating them as employees. This is WRONG, both morally and professionally, and it directly contravenes the systems and rules that society has put in place to protect workers' rights. The teachers can be put in a difficult position and may be bound to staying in a relationship with a studio even if they do not feel valued.

For example, one of my clients in the United States was told by the biggest yoga studio in his town that if he took a week off to lead a retreat, they would take away two of his weekly classes that he had held for years. In addition, they threatened to terminate his contractor agreement if he ran one of his own workshops at the same time as one of the studio's workshops. This is, plainly put, bullying. But in addition, it is also illegal. The studio was trying to enforce rights against a contractor that they would have had with an *employee* (vacation time, non-competition). I was aghast when this teacher hired me to help him stand up for himself and defend his rights. After a bit of investigation, I found that such scenarios were not all that uncommon.

I would say that scenarios like the one my client faced are still the exception instead of the rule, but in my opinion they should not exist at all. Everyone deserves to feel valued in their work. Even if people are not valued in their work, they deserve the *appropriate and fair protections provided* to them by law.

Story #1: The Audit (Cue the Scary Music)

This is a real story about one of my clients. It happened before I was retained to work for him – luckily for me, as it did not sound like it was a lot of fun. The client retained me after he went through the drawn-out, stressful and expensive experience of dealing with an audit. Remember the "pay me now, pay me later" thing? This was a pay me later. It only took one conversation to find out how badly this person wished he had set things up properly from the start. But now his lesson is all of our lesson, so we do not have to make the same mistakes.

I first met Terry at a yoga festival in Whistler and we became buddies right from the start. (I am sure you can see a pattern in how I make my friends.) We took some silly yoga class for guys called "Dude, Where's My Mat?" and found each other as partners in one of the early exercises. We were bros right away, which is always a good sign, and we kept bumping into each other over the course of the weekend. The highlight was jamming out together at an epic outdoor concert. We wanted to keep going after the show when all of our friends went to crash. Terry and I looked for a party but found a spot in the grass under the stars, and without speaking a word, we knew that this was where our after-hang would be. The stars… way better than any party out there.

From the second we hit the ground, our eyes tilted up at the sky, we started talking and did not stop until the sun came up. Terry told me everything about him. He had opened a yoga studio in Richmond, British Columbia and had just celebrated the studio's five-year anniversary. He told me the crazy story of his parents taking a mortgage out on their house to raise capital for him to start the venture, and how he went on to fully repay them and build a thriving business. He told me the tragic story of a student at his yoga studio who had committed suicide and had come to his class a few days before taking her life. "It broke my heart. And it reminded me of the great responsibility that I have as a community leader," he said stoically but solemnly. He told me of all the successes and the failures, the lessons learned and the opportunities for the future. Listening to him speak, I felt anything was possible if we willed it with our minds.

When we got to speaking about me, I witnessed Terry's rare and powerful gift of understanding people and their stories. After I shared with him what I was up to, it was clear from his first remarks that he would be my coach. At that time

I had a lot of doubts about my ability to carve out a path for myself, and it was his words that served as the impetus for me to become the person I am today. I will never forget his response when I voiced concerns about being able to work as a lawyer and be happy. He turned to me and looked deep into my eyes. "You have a powerful voice," he said. "Find out what you want to say and people will listen." I have chills even as I write this out now, remembering the moment so vividly. It was one of the moments in my life that I will never forget.

When I told Terry my ideas about Yoga Law, he responded in a frustrated voice: "Oh man, I really could have used you last year when I got audited." I inquired to hear more. Terry took a deep breath and began the story. "Well, basically we had a teacher on our staff who did not pay his taxes. He wasn't really a great teacher and I should have known something was up with him. It just so happened that this guy didn't pay his taxes for three years – and was working multiple jobs in and out of yoga. I think he did graphic design stuff on the side as well. Anyways, we got a letter from the CRA (Canadian Revenue Agency) that said they had some questions about our working relationship with him. It seems that once he got busted for not paying his taxes, the natural defence was to claim that he was an employee of our yoga studio and thought we were deducting the taxes for him. We both knew that was a lie, but he was clearly doing anything he could to protect himself."

I stared in disbelief. I had only been a lawyer for a few months at this point, and I had not really touched on any employment law stuff yet. I was so curious. "What happened?" I asked. "It wasn't fun," he continued, *almost* smiling, indicating that he was happy the whole ordeal was behind him. "We got audited. The CRA determined that he was an employee based on the work he was doing for us and we got dinged for over

$30,000 in back taxes and penalties. I was shocked! I had no idea we were so exposed. Worst of all, I was so close to paying my dad back around that time and it took me nearly a year to recover." Any of my other friends would have lost it and gotten angry at this point, but I saw Terry's true yogic spirit emerge. "But," he said, "it was all part of my journey and I am better for the experience." DAMN, I thought. This guy is legit.

We went on to speak about the little I knew of the law that could be helpful to him and his business. As we prepared to shift off the topic, he said, "Let me know when you get Yoga Law off the ground and I'll be your first client. Clearly, I need to understand my contracts with my staff." And true to his word, when the day came that I sent him a link to my Yoga Law website, Terry responded immediately and asked if I was ready to go. Before I could even muster a "hello" over the phone, he said: "Namaste bro. Let's do this." I chuckled to myself, thinking that this was why I loved doing work with yogis – they are just special people.

Terry taught me a few important lessons. His encouragement to use my voice proved to be a breakthrough that led me to where I am and what I am doing today. But in our conversation, he also showed me how a lot of yoga studio owners did not understand the difference between contractors and employees, and how they could be exposed to risk as a result of their ignorance. (I had many subsequent conversations with studio owners and teachers about his story, all of which corroborated my thesis that no one is really aware of this difference.) It was clear from Terry's tale that this information needed to be shared, and I am glad to do so here.

Story #2: The Taco Tax Party

While I am sure that everyone has heard of the Boston Tea Party of 1773, I cannot help but wonder if anyone has heard of the lesser-known and historically irrelevant Santa Cruz Tax Party that took place at a yoga studio in Santa Cruz, California? This is a cute little story about one of my clients that illustrates a practical way studio owners can work with their staff to ensure that everyone pays their taxes. Whether you are a contractor or not, having someone remind you to do your taxes properly is a good thing.

It was just after sunset on a beautiful night in the third week of April. A yoga studio owner sat on a block surrounded by her entire team of staff. The agenda for the night involved a brief meeting and then a feast of vegan tacos from Taqueria Los Pericos. Party favours were strewn from the ceiling and the studio owner was donning a party hat, possibly from her daughter's third birthday party that had passed the week before. She called attention to the room. All conversations came to a hush and all eyes focused on the leader. "Okay team," she said emphatically, "I want to start this party just as bad as you do – and I can already taste the guacamole awaiting us outside. *Show me your tax returns* and we can start this party."

You might be scratching your head as you read this, so let me provide a bit of context. I had given a talk on Yoga Law at Wanderlust and met some awesome yoga teachers and studio owners afterwards. I kept in touch with a bunch of them who had a lot of really good questions about their business. One of them was a lovely and ambitious business professional turned yoga teacher who had aspirations to open her own studio. She was from Santa Cruz and her name was Miranda. Miranda was passionate about her vision, clear on what she wanted and ambitious enough to make it happen.

Miranda sent me an email a few weeks after the Wanderlust talk asking for some help. I told her that I was not allowed to practice law in California and knew nothing about laws in that state, but I could offer advice on general legal principles. We spoke generally about the plan she had set up to take over the studio, and then she expressed concern about being held responsible if the studio's teachers were incorrectly classified as contractors by the previous owner, knowing she'd have to foot the bill later down the line. She had heard me tell Terry's story at Wanderlust and now she wanted to be proactive to ensure that she avoided any such headaches or holes in her pockets.

The first thing I told Miranda was that the she needed to make sure the seller of the studio would agree to be personally responsible in the event that the studio had misclassified its working relationships. In addition, I advised Miranda not to pay the full purchase price upfront and instead pay it over an extended period of time. The purpose of this was to keep some leverage and create a buffer to make sure that if she did need to pay back taxes, interest or penalties, she could do so from the purchase price instead of having to hassle the seller for the money.

The second thing we discussed was the importance of communicating with her staff about what it meant to be an employee or an independent contractor – and how it affected them not only in the studio but also in their life. At her studio, she had contractors (yoga teachers and workshop leaders) and employees (staff who consistently worked at the studio in 9–5 type jobs). I gave her a bit of a primer on the basic points she needed to highlight for her staff. At least now, her staff would know what they should be doing and would be more likely to do it. We also re-worked Miranda's contractor agreements to make sure that she was asking her teachers to do tasks that were in fact the tasks of a contractor and not an employee.

Miranda's next concern moving forward was how to be sure that her contractors would in fact pay their taxes. To fix this problem, we simply came up with the rule that any contractor who worked for her would have to prove that they paid their taxes and specifically declared the amount they had been paid by the studio. She would make this a *precondition* for anyone who wanted to work in her studio as a contractor. While some people may find such a practice invasive, it is incredibly practical. It was also an excellent way for Miranda to safeguard herself from liability. From our perspective, she was taking on a risk by running the studio and was able to create rules for how she did things in her place.

I told Miranda that what would matter the most would be the way she communicated this request to her staff. It was all in the packaging. Instead of taking an authoritative position and demanding personal and private information, *she should let her team know where she was coming from and why she was coming from that place.*

I thought a bit about Santa Cruz, a beautiful Northern California town that was famous for good waves and invariably delicious Mexican food. "Why don't you have a taco tax party?" I asked, as if it was a real thing. There was silence on the other end of the phone. "Never heard of it," she said. The idea was forming in my brain as the words were coming out of my mouth. "Why don't you call a staff meeting but call it a Taco Tax party. Do it after everyone has filed their taxes and received their tax returns so that you can see they have declared the amount you paid them from the studio. Make it a super fun night to get people excited about it, decorate the studio and cancel classes for the night so that everyone can be together. It can be a bonding experience for your team, too." Her first reaction was, "I love it." She exclaimed, "Oh my god, I know exactly what music I am going to play." She ended up throwing the party and then sent me a thank-you note with a picture of the group smiling.

The Taco Tax Party illustrates how we can find creative ways to work with the law. If we look at the basic legal issue at hand, it can seem very boring and mundane. But when you realize what is at stake and what can happen if you slip up, you finally become interested. Once you are interested, the next step is getting educated and executing a plan in an enjoyable manner. When margaritas, tacos and Buena Vista Social Club are involved, who doesn't want to be there?

Please note that Miranda's Taco Tax Party was not a foolproof plan. There was no guarantee that she would totally avoid issues that could arise with her independent contractors and employees. I was never hired to help with her worker classifications, and instead just practically shared my understanding of the law. But Miranda put herself in a *much better position to succeed* by taking great strides to understand the legal issues and inform her team about them. A similar effort could catch 90 percent of problems before they arise, and that is the whole point of this book and Yoga Law in general. I am not detailing all of the legal nuances and my suggestions are not perfect. But my suggestions will at least give you something practical and help you understand things that you need to be aware of. Plus, you may even decide to eat a taco after reading this story, in which case it would be a *win-win*.

Practical Points: Crafting Agreements for Independent Contractors

As we know from this chapter, the biggest factor in determining whether or not someone is a contractor or employee is the degree of control you have over the services they provide. You could have two workers providing the same service, but if they are offering it in different ways then they could be classified in two different ways. This is one of the greatest value propositions that lawyers offer: They can craft an agreement in which a yoga teacher will work for you in a way that makes them either a contractor or employee. Below are a few things that I usually do in agreements to create a contractor relationship instead of an employee relationship. This process only takes place once I have determined that the staff can in fact be contractors and that the client is not trying to contravene any relevant laws.

- Start with the mentality that the workers operate their own business and that the studio owner is simply *contracting out* a service for the studio. This is the whole point of working with a contractor.
- Give the workers as much freedom as possible in performing their services. For example, if they are teaching yoga, the agreement does not tell them what type of yoga to teach or how they should teach their classes.
- Avoid too many restrictive provisions in the agreement.
- Ask the worker to send in invoices in order to get paid.
- Ensure that the workers use their own equipment and materials as much as possible when they are providing their services. For example, they will wear their own clothes, play their own music from their own phone, and even bring their own mat.

- Avoid asking workers to do things that an employee would normally do, such as work the front desk, clean the studio after class and sell goods at the studio shop. Similarly, avoid asking workers to do things outside the normal scope of their services.
- Avoid giving workers guaranteed places on the schedule, which is a tell-tale sign of an employee. Ideally, the worker would provide their services wherever and whenever they want, but in yoga that is not possible. One option is to ask the worker every month which times they would prefer to teach (less control) instead of pre-assigning class times that they must cover (more control).

Your Chapter Checklist:

Here are the key points to remember about employees and contractors:

- It doesn't matter what you call your workers, it matters what type of work they do for you and the way that they do it.
- Typically, one will be an employee when you exercise more control on the way they provide services for you. Conversely, think of contractors as people who run their own business and whom you hire to provide a service for your business.
- You'll retain the IP rights in something an employee creates for you (as long it is in the normal course of their employment) but at law, you will not have exclusive rights to the creation of a contractor unless agreed so.
- You run the risk of getting audited if you misclassify employees as contractors or do not properly pay all your employee's taxes.

Chapter 7

Building Your Brand, Protecting Your Assets

Intention

In this chapter, we will look at how the law of intellectual property (IP) can help you protect your business assets. IP law protects an individual's unique creations and artistic works. Without it, people could just copy each other's ideas and no one would be rewarded for coming up with anything unique on their own. For the purposes of Yoga Law, we are going to focus on the relevant aspects of copyright, trademark and licensing. Before we get there, however, I am going to start with a brief discussion about reverse engineering, branding and active/passive income, because it is imperative to understand these concepts before you set off building your business. If you have already built your business, this discussion will provide great reminders to course correct and ensure that you are on your path to success, as defined only by you.

If you remember only one thing from this chapter, remember that if something is yours, protect it. This will be the key to the growth of your business and your income, whether active or passive. Read the story at the end of this chapter to learn best practices in this field ("Story: The Ideal Success Story").

Part I: Building Your Brand

Reverse Engineering

Reverse engineering is a concept that really excites me, and one that I credit for empowering me to build my business online. Some books call this concept "starting with the end in mind," but I feel that reverse engineering captures the spirit of the initiative in a more pragmatic way. Reverse engineering means that you simply build something backwards. You start with a very clear idea of how your finished product will look (you living in a small home with picket fences, a yellow lab, a beautiful partner and two kids, a kickass business you can operate from any coffee shop in the world, a yoga practice that helps you touch your toes), and then you work backwards to bring it to reality. The key to executing this properly is that *every single decision you make has to be aligned with your intended outcome.*

It makes sense to place the concept of reverse engineering in this chapter because my discussions of IP will focus mostly on growing, building and protecting your brand. The concept is related to IP because you should have a very clear vision of your brand – what it is and how people feel about it – before you create it. And then you create, protect and grow it by solidifying and registering the appropriate IP tools.

I first practiced reverse engineering when I decided to take my legal business online. "A law firm existing online?" people would say to me. "It will never work." Obviously, I did not care or listen to what other people said, as is evidenced by the fact that I am editing this book on a beach in Brazil, where I peer my head up from the screen to see the sunrise and incredible ocean. I knew that I could make it work and that I would not have a fully expressed business if I were limited to living in one city. My dream was and still is to travel the world and build my business. There is no time like the present, so I just did it. I learned that when you are determined to make something work for your life, you propel past stories of why it should not work and simply make it work. The wrong people fall away and the right ones emerge from the woodwork to help you on your path. The Universe is always supporting you, whether or not you can see it that way or not.

Through the entire process (which is still ongoing), every decision that I have made about my business has been pitted against the following question: "Will this decision help me achieve my goal of building a thriving business that I can operate from anywhere in the world?" That is reverse engineering in a nutshell. When you reverse engineer and get clear about what you want, you can simply crosscheck every decision you make about your business against where you want to end up.

So, in case you have never done this or you have not done it in a while, take a moment to meditate, breathe and think about how your business ends. Go ahead. Set a timer for five minutes and just breathe into your dream. Visualize where you are, who is there with you, what you are doing and how you are helping people. Is it a retreat space on Galiano Island? Is it having your classes at studios all across the country? Is it you travelling the world and teaching at different festivals in different countries? Is it you teaching at your favourite studio just down the street? Once the five minutes are up, write down as much as you want about what you saw – it could be a word or a few pages. Once you know where you are going, it will be easier to make the appropriate decisions on how to get there.

Active/Passive Income

As a prelude to any discussion of IP law in relation to branding and marketing, I would like to turn your attention to the difference between active and passive income. Active income is money that you earn when you personally carry out services. Examples of this would be the money you earn when you teach a class at a studio, or when you lead a retreat or facilitate a teaching training. By contrast, passive income is money that you earn when something you have set up performs a service that operates itself without you. Examples of this would be owning a yoga studio that does not need you to carry out its day-to-day operations, or having a teacher pay you a licensing fee in order to teach your particular methods when they lead a teaching training of a method you've started.

Passive income is super juicy because it enables you to make money without having to do anything. You build something that allows you to go hiking in Hawaii while students flock to your studio in your hometown or a student in Singapore buys your workshops online. By no means should you aspire to generate passive income unless you really want to, but it is a common goal of entrepreneurs because it allows them to earn money while doing whatever they want. I just want to plant this little seed into your mind because a lot of yogis do not actively turn their minds to setting up passive income. Reverse engineer your life – if passive income is what you want, be aware of it from the beginning and build accordingly.

Scaling Your Business + Your Unique Offering

If there is one aspect of entrepreneurism in which I have seen yogis lack significant foresight, it is directing their minds to scaling their business. I would like to address this concept here, because scaling your business goes hand in hand with your IP.

Scaling your business means building and expanding your business so that it becomes bigger than just you. I have so many friends and teachers who burn out as yoga teachers because they teach fifteen studio classes a week and never stop to think about how they can grow their business. They are *in* their business instead of working on their business (feel free to read the book "The E-Myth" for an expansion on this idea). Even when I ask them about their plans to scale, they often cannot wrap their head around the concept. And I understand why – they have always thought that working as a yoga teacher just meant teaching studio classes.

For the moment, the only thing about scaling that I want you to acknowledge is that you can take your special offering and expand the world's exposure to it. You can do this online or you can do it in real physical spaces. But all of this depends on you having a *unique offering*. This means that you have to create something that is done uniquely your way. You create it and you make it yours. Once it has been created and people have fallen in love with it, you scale it so that it becomes available to as many people as possible.

How do you create your unique offering in yoga? Hasn't everything already been done? Absolutely not! There is only space for creation. The yoga "industry" is still quite young. As long as you make your own contribution to how this beautiful practice can be offered and enjoyed, you can build a business that can be scaled. Again, if this is not your intention, there is no problem with that. But most of the yoga professionals I speak to and work with would love to be in a position to scale. The connection between scaling and IP is clear: You scale with your unique idea or offering, and then you use IP laws to protect the unique idea or offering. This is why we are here.

Branding: How the World Sees You before They Meet You

Your brand is one of the most important things for your business in the year 2019, second only to the quality of the services you provide. What you do and how you do it are the services you provide. The way people perceive your business and feel about it when they are not directly interacting with it is your branding. Your branding tells people who you are, what you do, why and how you do it, and how much they are going to love it. Every word must be surgically placed with precision, every aspect of your design deeply contemplated.

To understand the power of branding, and thus the need to be legally sound in this area, I will ask you to observe some of your own commercial behaviour. Think about how many times you make a decision purely based on how something looks or makes you feel, even though you have never actually seen it or used it. You go to an Instagram account or a website and start snooping around. Suddenly, you are inundated with images and words about the experience of a product that you actually know nothing about, except what the images and words choose to tell you. Then you create expectations in your mind about what the experience will be like and get carried away. This is why we pay so much money for clothes, gym memberships and cars. It is not about what we are using, it is about how we feel when using it.

How do you sell five hundred tickets to an event that does not exist? Yep, you got it. You make a great website, have a cool logo and create an online experience that will direct people to how you want them to feel. How do you start a law firm online and attract clients from around the world while working from the beaches of Tel Aviv or the banks of the Ganges? You tell people how you want them to feel about your service or product and then follow through when you interact with them.

If you are interested in learning more about branding, read anything by Seth Godin. He totally gets it and uses a simple yet insanely intelligent approach to explain how marketing and branding work. His book *The Purple Cow* greatly impacted me. In one of his books, when discussing health foods and branding, he rhetorically asks: Who suddenly decided that granola is healthy? The question is so simple but explains everything. Granola is not necessarily a good food choice, but we are told that it is, so we believe it. Then we automatically order it without considering how much sugar it may contain compared to, let's say, plain oats.

I will never forget the time I met with a potential client in the early days of running my own business. We had swapped a few emails and decided to grab a coffee in the Coal Harbour area of Vancouver to see if working together could be a fit. As we sat down, me with an americano and she with an espresso, she immediately blurted out: "Oh my god, I am so happy I found you." I responded, "Thank you," cautiously and confused. She continued: "I went on your website and realized that I totally understand you. I really, really get what you are about and how you work. I know that I want to work with you because I get you. I know what I want to do in business and I know we are going to be great together." I was shocked. I actually had no idea what to say. "Well, it's all true," I said with an impish grin as we both laughed aloud. We ended up having a great meeting and are still working together fruitfully today.

When I hopped on my bike after the meeting, I could not

help but think about how strange it all was. I had projected an image to the world about my ethos, why I do what I do and how I do it, and people had really connected with it without meeting me. I suppose all of this is just second nature to me, because I am being super authentic in what I do. But it is still scarily impressive how powerful marketing and branding can be. In fact, I have fallen in love twice over Instagram (both were disasters) and each experience taught me a great deal about consumer behaviour – the effect of calculated, potentially misleading text coupled with beautiful imagery. We are all branding and marketing ourselves all the time, and the sooner we grasp this, the more consistent and intentional we can be with the message we put out to the world.

PART II: Protecting Your Assets

The Need for IP

The need to build your business around your brand is real. If you *want to grow your business once it is built,* you are most likely going to do so around your brand, which will consist of a logo, a slogan and your own creative works. Examples of creative works in this context can be coming up with your own yoga methodology or writing a teacher training course. The value of these creations goes only so far as they are protected at law. The law works behind the scenes to secure all of your rights and ideas associated with your brand, enabling you to leverage the value of these properties to do whatever you want to do. There is a twofold rationale behind all IP laws: Firstly, reward and recognize people for creating awesome things, and secondly, prevent people misleading the public about who originally created an idea or artistic work.

Trademark

For clarity's sake, any time that I refer to a "mark" or "the mark," I am referring to an example of something that you would register for a trademark. For example, a word like Nike, a series of words used together like Just Do It, or a symbol like the Nike checkmark.

The reason why trademarks exist: Governments created trademark registration to let people protect their IP and to protect the public from being misled. Think about it – if there were no rules governing how people could use logos or designs, how would we know who produced the products we are buying? If the marketplace was a free-for-all and anyone could just copy Nike's checkmark symbol on their clothes, how would we know what is real and what is fake? Furthermore, why would anyone come up with a cool new idea if they knew that anyone else could just rip it off?

Protection: Governments desperately want to protect and give mad props to business owners and individuals who come up with great logos or slogans that set their brand apart from the rest. They want to set you up so that no one else can copy what you use to distinguish your brand from the rest of the world. By registering a mark, you empower yourself with the right to stop someone from using words or logos that infringe on what you created or started using first. You get to write that person a letter saying, "Nice try, but I'm the one who came up with this first so kindly stop using a logo that looks exactly like mine."

Public confusion: In addition to protecting business owners and creative individuals, governments also want to safeguard the public from being misled by sneaky copiers. If there were no trademark laws, the public could easily be misled about where products come from and who really produced the services or goods they are consuming.

Scope of registration: It is important to know that once you register a mark, you do not get unlimited use of it across all fields. You have to specify exactly how you have used the mark or plan to use the mark. You are only granted exclusive rights for the areas in which you use the mark. This is why there can be several companies named "Jiffy," all of which operate in different industries. The key when registering your mark is to be as specific as possible about how you want to use the mark to ensure that you get to use it where you really need it.

Registered vs. unregistered: Just because you have not officially registered a mark does not mean that you have no rights in it. In Canada, if you are the first person to use a mark in business, you start off with the best rights. But, if you do not act on these rights and register your mark, someone else can. Once they begin the trademark process (explained below), they are already ahead in the race. The worst-case scenario is that they successfully complete the trademark registration process and gain exclusive rights to use the trademark, prohibiting from you using it. At this point, you can challenge the trademark on the basis that you used it first, but this will cost a lot of cash and take a lot of time. If you have built your brand around this mark, do not wait for someone else to register it. You get rewarded for being proactive, so get after it.

Takeaway: If you have a mark that everyone uses to identify your goods or services, it could be helpful to register it as a trademark. Remember, this is about protecting and exercising your rights. The whole point of registering a trademark is that you are telling the world, "Hey, I am the only person allowed to use my logo/slogan, because when people see it they'll think the product they are getting is from me." Trademark registration is about protecting exclusive use of your words/designs, so that someone else will not use them to confuse the public, and so that you are rewarded for creating something awesome that the public can identify as yours.

When Does It Make Sense to Register a Trademark?

This is a common question that I hear from clients. "Do I even need to register for a trademark?" It is a good question. There are certainly times when it is beneficial to do so and other times when it is less pressing. There is no uniform answer and the decision to register is based on a number of factors. I will give a couple of examples below that explain when it may or may not make sense to register, and hopefully this will turn your mind in the right direction for your mark and what you have created.

Example 1

I started a business called Conscious Counsel. The name was great and I had not seen anyone else using it in the market. I did my research and saw that there was nothing similar registered in the trademark registry. I applied to have the words *Conscious Counsel* trademarked for my exclusive use in the realm of legal services, amongst other things. The process was completed over the course of eighteen months, and then I became the only person in Canada allowed to use the term Conscious Counsel in my chosen fields for the next fifteen years.

Explanation: Registering a unique name like Conscious Counsel is a no-brainer. The name is hot and it is a great idea. Due credit must be given to my client-turned-friend Shayna Grimwood, who told me at a Victoria health food conference, "You are like a conscious counsellor." Thanks Shay! If I did not register this name, I could see someone else doing it. So, I locked it down. If I had not registered and protected the mark, someone else *could* have registered it and prevented me from using the name Conscious Counsel. That would have been devastating because I have built my entire business and brand around the name.

Takeaway: If you have got a great name or slogan that people use to identify your business, consider protecting it now. In addition to being the only person who gets to use a protected mark, you can make money from licensing it out in the future, a.k.a. getting people to pay for using your IP.

Example 2

My wonderful and talented friend Sam Rozon came up with the design for the Conscious Counsel logo in January 2017, just as I was kicking off the business. It is a beautiful triangle (the shape of shapes) and has simple yet cool lettering. I love how it looks. In spite of this, I have decided not to register it as a trademark, because there is very little risk in losing it and because it does not play an integral part in my business. I do not believe that people see the logo and identify it with my business.

For example, *if* I were to receive a letter tomorrow telling me that my logo looked exactly like a logo someone else had used first and that I had to change it, I would not be too bothered. I do not pay for advertising; I do not put my logo up in a physical location; and my brand is built upon the words *Conscious Counsel* rather than my logo. I am not certain that I will keep this logo forever, but I am certainly using the words *Conscious Counsel* to build several businesses.

Just as an example, I might choose to trademark my logo if my business involved selling apparel and people specifically sought out products with my logo on it – especially if my logo stood for something elite, expensive or cool. Think of lululemon, Manduka or Gaia Inc. These are all consumer brands that are built around people recognizing their logo, paying a premium for their products and associating a certain feeling or quality with the product. As such, it is imperative for these companies to register their logos.

Takeaway: If people identify your brand with a particular logo, and if they will in fact purchase your goods/services partly because of that logo, consider registering the logo as a trademark immediately. You want to be in full control of such a valuable asset if it drives your business.

Example 3

Let's say you are a yoga teacher who is well known and teaches at some of the biggest studios in your hometown. You do not plan to open your own studio and you are quite content running a couple of retreats and teaching studio classes. You use your name for your business with a logo that your friend made of your initials in a swirly, hipster-looking design. You do not have a slogan that people identify with your business, because people mostly know you by name, by your Instagram or by your reputation in the city. Should you trademark any of your assets?

In this scenario, I would say probably not. What drives your business is not your name or your logo, but instead you. You cannot trademark a person's name (see the FAQ below) and people do not identify your personal yoga services with your logo. They know you because they know you in person, or they know of you, or you teach their best friend who is in love with you. On this level, there really is nothing that needs to be trademarked because the implications of someone copying your logo are small, and because no one else can use your name for their business.

Takeaway: You want to trademark slogans, words or particulars that are assets for your business. If you are running a successful yoga business and none of these things drive your business (it happens), you risk nothing by losing them and should feel no pressure to trademark them. Acquiring exclusive rights to use something of little value will not help you as you achieve your goals.

FAQ: Trademarks

Question 1: What If I Come Up with a Great Slogan, Don't Register It and Someone Else Does?

Answer: In Canada, the person who initially has the best rights to a mark is the one who used it first. Registration provides additional benefits and the government wants to reward people for registering. So, while you do have the best rights in the mark initially, someone else can register the mark or a similar mark if you have not acted quickly enough. Once someone else is registered and you are unregistered, you are fighting an uphill battle even if you used the mark first. The system rewards proactive businesses people, so if you snooze you lose.

Question 2: What Can Be Trademarked?

Answer: A word, a series of words, a sound or a design can be trademarked. The word or words can be the name of your business, so long as the public identifies your business by that name. The purpose is to register a mark that distinguishes your goods or services from the world at large and thereby avoid public confusion.

Question 3: What Cannot Be Trademarked?

Answer: The following cannot be trademarked:
- People's names – it's not cool to other people who have that name, you know?! For example, Baron Baptiste cannot be trademarked but Baron Baptiste Yoga could work.
- Words in other languages – for example, namaste means "hello" in Nepalese. However, you can trademark words in other languages so long as they are accompanied by other words and you understand you'll never have exclusive use of a word itself in another language.
- Places of origin – the idea is that you do not get to be the only person to say that you make a certain product from a certain place. For example, Italy as a trademark for a pasta would not work.
- Words or designs that could be confused with a registered or pending trademark.
- Anything that misleads the public – for example, Yin Yoga Adventures (sounds fun, actually) if you do not offer yin yoga.
- Descriptive marks – you cannot register a word that describes a feature of your goods or services. For example, Relaxing Savasana would not be registrable.

Question 4: How Long Does It Last?

Answer: A trademark registration is valid for fifteen years in Canada and ten years in the United States. After this period, a registration should be renewed if the trademark is still in use.

Copyright

Copyright is a fairly straightforward area of law that can be very relevant to yoga business owners and professionals. Whenever you create an original literary, dramatic, musical or artistic work, you automatically have the exclusive copyright in it. Basically, this means that you have created something original and automatically have the exclusive right to decide how the material will be used or not used in the future. Once you create it, it is yours. And, just to be clear here, having the idea in your head doesn't mean you've created it. It needs to be in a tangible form to be eligible for copyright.

Copyright law is very important in the entertainment industry, but it also plays its own part for health and wellness professionals. For the purposes of Yoga Law, we are going to look at copyright in the context of original creations (teacher training documents, manuals and website content). I will address some common issues that always seem to pop up for my clients. I will also briefly address the Bikram Yoga copyright case which took place in the State of New York from 2011, which sheds light on the question of whether or not one can copyright yoga poses. Throughout, I will explain things that you can do to put yourself and your copyright in the best positions to succeed, and I will provide tips for how you can use copyright to build and protect your business.

FAQ: Copyright

Question 1: When Are the Rights in Copyright Created?

Answer: The moment that you create something! For example, I have copyright in this book and everything that I write in it as I type it out. The rights exist automatically upon creation.

Question 2: So, Why Register a Copyright?

Answer: When you register a copyright, you show that you have the best evidence possible that you own the rights in what you have created. This is very helpful if you think someone else will try to use your materials. It is also helpful because you can clearly define all of the copyrighted materials you license out with an official copyright certificate number. In addition, registering a copyright is a rather straightforward process. But please note that the lack of a copyright certificate does not mean you do not have rights in your work.

Question 3: How Long Does Copyright Last?

Answer: In Canada, copyright generally lasts for the lifetime of the creator and then fifty years following their death. At that point, the copyright is considered to be in the public domain. In the United States, copyright lasts for the lifetime of the creator and then seventy years following their death.

Question 4: What Is Covered under Copyright?

Answer: The creation of literary, artistic, dramatic and musical works. For example, this would include a book, a dance, a song or a photograph.

Question 5: Can You Copyright Yoga Asanas?

Answer: No, you cannot. We learned this in the Bikram Yoga story which took place in the United States. Bikram Choudhury tried to prevent other yoga studios in the State of New York from performing parts of his hot yoga sequences, claiming that while he did not create the poses himself, he created the sequence in which they were used for specific health benefits. Ultimately, the courts ruled that he was unable to copyright his sequences, and thus everyone was allowed to use yoga poses in any sequence they desired (as they should be).

Story: Copyright Issue

My most memorable story about copyright issues is not such a positive one, but it does have a hopeful resolution. I was hired by a yoga studio that wanted to firm up their legal agreements because they were about to embark on a new venture, growing their brand by continuously offering teacher trainings at the studio. They had ambitions for an academy. My clients were named Willy and Rae. They were not yoga teachers themselves and had never completed a teacher training, but they loved the community and wanted to get involved. Their intentions were good.

Before they retained me, my clients had run one teacher training course at their studio. They had hired a teacher named Carmen to lead the course, who regularly taught at the studio and who had led teacher trainings in the past. Carmen served almost as a consultant in her role, explaining to the studio how to run a teacher training and contributing important materials to the teacher-training handbook. My clients had a small group of students signed up and Carmen did not bring in any additional students. They offered an excellent course and felt that they were well on their way to having the yoga training program they wanted.

When my clients retained me, the first thing I asked them for was a chance to peruse through their documents pertaining to the yoga teacher training. I had expected to see agreements with their students and a contractor agreement with Carmen. I was a bit worried but certainly not surprised when I learned that Willy and Rae had no existing agreements. "That's why you are here," Rae said to me, with a bubbly giggle as she gave me a big hug. And the truth is, Rae was right.

Up to this point in time, Willy and Rae had run only one teacher training and had luckily escaped without any injuries or problems – or so it seemed. I drafted a teacher training student agreement for their incoming students and an independent contractor agreement for Carmen. "Oh, we won't need that," Willy said confidently. "Carmen has moved to another city and won't be helping us out any longer." At this point, I did not know that Carmen had contributed to the teacher training handbook and trusted Willy that all was well on that front.

Willy and Rae's business took off, seemingly out of nowhere. Willy was a marketing whiz and Rae and was excellent at running a business. Together, they were able to bring their vision of a yoga academy to fruition. People loved it, the business had integrity, the training was taught thoroughly, and Willy and Rae were empowering people to bring more yoga to the world. They were using the agreements I had drafted for them and everything looked in order. From all appearances, it was a straightforward situation of course correcting my clients to best legal practices and then being on my way.

All that changed when I got a frantic phone call from the usually light and relaxed Rae. "We just got an email from Carmen. She says that she is demanding money from our teacher training because she wrote most of our teacher-training manual. She is asking to see our financials to determine how much she is owed. I've forwarded you her email. This can't be happening," Rae said almost in shock. I reassured her that everything would be okay and told her to keep breathing. I quickly hung up the phone and ran to my computer.

I reviewed Carmen's email and – legally speaking – she was right. She said that she had created most of the materials the academy was using. While she no longer led the teaching, she had still given them the foundation to build their academy – and they had done exactly that. She was hired by the studio to organize the teacher training and to create specific content and processes for how the training would run (which Willy and Rae still used). When she was hired as a contractor, Carmen never agreed to relinquish ownership in the materials she created.

I met with Willy and Rae after a delicious seventy-five-minute yin class at their studio. In a very calm demeanour, I explained their position: "The way it works with copyright is that if Carmen helped write part of the materials you are using, and if when you paid her *you didn't explicitly agree that you were purchasing full ownership in the materials*, then she owns half. The situation is complicated but the principle is clear." I was trying to be as forthright as possible.

"But she wants so much money," Willy exclaimed. "We were the ones who did all the marketing to bring in these students who paid for the course. How much is she actually entitled to?" In true lawyering fashion, I replied, "It depends," and slowly continued. "She can make a lot of arguments that she should be entitled to half of what you've earned from the teaching. She could say that because the materials and processes are so good, people loved the course and told their friends. In a practical sense, I think we should speak with her and come to a compromise that we both feel is fair."

Willy and Rae looked at each other. "I am willing to do that. But, what is frustrating is that Carmen knew our intentions and also knew she wasn't going to stick around. I really thought there was an understanding we were paying her a one-time payment and then it would be our project." I could see that Willy was frustrated, so I responded: "I know – and I really do get you brother. But we would need that information in writing or with some form of support. If you thought that on your own and didn't communicate it, we could never prove it was part of the deal."

Rae looked at me and suddenly her smile reappeared. "Okay, lesson learned. Let's settle this and move forward," she said. We hugged and then I hopped on my bike and rode to my favourite Japanese restaurant, Shizenya, to get to work.

In the end, the negotiations went smoothly and closed quickly. It was easy for me because Carmen was simply looking for a fair deal, and my clients were willing to pay and wanted to move on. No animosity, just straight business. We arrived at a number that worked for everyone and while it did cost my clients money, they learned an important lesson. Most importantly, in exchange for my clients' payment, we had Carmen sign an agreement that assigned all IP to my clients. They now exclusively owned their teacher training program.

I was very proud of Willy and Rae because they had not let this issue affect them negatively, and had adopted the mindset that they should just improve their business to cover whatever paying Carmen would cost. And, that is just what they did. Their academy continues to thrive and I applaud them for being proactive in working with the law, rather than waiting too long to do so and not sweating the small stuff. What could have been a major strain turned out to be a success story.

Licensing

Licensing is a super juicy of area of law that I love telling my clients about. In plain English, licensing is when someone pays you (or offers something else of value) for using IP that you have created. The beauty of licensing is that it rewards you for your creations by growing and scaling your business, bringing the creations to life and protecting your IP. There are all sorts of different types of licenses (exclusive vs. non-exclusive, ability to change the IP, fixed period vs. in perpetuity).

The important concept to grasp is that whether you are paying someone to use their IP or vice versa, *licensing is created around definable IP*. I highlight this because it illustrates a critical concept that I need you to grasp: You need to have definable or recognizable IP in order to license it out. If you have not put your ducks in a row and organized your copyright or trademark rights, it will not matter how amazing your idea is or how cool your concept is, because you will not be able to properly scale it. Are you with me here? Can you grasp the significance of setting things up appropriately if you want to grow?

Ideally, this is how the process should look:
- Step 1: Ideation
- Step 2: Creation
- Step 3: Protection (securing IP rights)

- Step 4: Growth and Scale (licensing your IP rights on terms that serve you)

Now, what happens if these steps are not properly followed? Let's take the example of the teacher training materials in the copyright story from earlier in this chapter and dive a bit deeper. In that story, we saw how the teacher training organizers did not properly assert their ownership of the teacher-training manual. It was not clear that they hired the contractor to contribute to the teaching materials while intending to keep the IP for themselves. At law the contractor had IP rights in what was created. Accordingly, because the organizers did not clearly own the property, it would have been extremely difficult for them to license it out to a third party who might want such materials (unless the contractor agreed to let them do so).

So, even if the organizers in my story had co-created something amazing that was scalable around the whole world, they would have faced challenges licensing it. Why would they have faced challenges? No one will agree to pay a license fee to use someone else's awesome branding or creation unless it *actually belongs to that person*. They will want to make sure the person properly and entirely owns the branding or creation before they pay a penny for it. This is because they need to know that they are not at risk of a) illegally using someone else's IP, and b) losing all the money, time and effort of setting up the licensing structure in the first place. If you cannot prove you own the IP outright, no one will (or should) pay you anything for it.

This is all I really want you to understand about licensing. For the purpose of this book and your yoga career, I will skip the boring nuances and technicalities of licensing and just encourage you *to understand the need to properly secure your IP*

because it is the gateway to the next step of licensing out your IP.
Licensing can be the avenue to you achieving your dreams.

Story: The Ideal Success Story

Here is a cool story about a client who moved from ideation
to scaling and did it properly. The story illustrates how this can
be done correctly every step of the way – and what that looks
like in real life. It is one of the best examples I have seen of
a person utilizing IP to grow and develop a business toward
passive income. I am sharing it to show you the best practices
(in my opinion) for using trademark, copyright and licensing
agreements to lead a dream life.

I met Hadas one afternoon while I was hanging out with
some friends at Stinson Beach. I was back in San Francisco
visiting old friends from my time working at the Raiders and
a couple of other buddies who still called "The City" their
home. We arrived with a football, a frisbee and some Two-
Buck Chuck from Trader Joes. As we set up camp for the day,
I looked at the sunshine spread across this long, stretched-out
Northern Californian beach. "God, I miss this place," I thought
to myself. There is something about being Canadian that makes
you appreciate beautiful sunny weather that much more.

A few of us went for a quick jog in the sand to find the
flattest space for a football game. The wind was picking up and
my skin quickly grasped the salty air coming in from the ocean.
Less than two hundred metres into our journey, we heard
someone call out my buddy's name. "Jesse… is that you?" came
a voice from a group sitting off to the side. Jesse's ears perked
up and he squinted his eyes. "Linda… could it possibly be…
Lindaaaaaa!" he screamed. In less than a millisecond, he bolted
over to a group of girls sitting in the sand. I stood off to the side

with my buddy Nick waiting for Jesse to return, but he did not come back. Jesse grabbed a beer and sat down beside Linda. So long football game! We walked over and introduced ourselves to the group. Jesse had forgotten to introduce us, clearly too captivated by this chance meeting with Linda. He was in the position – laying on his side facing Linda, giving her his full attention. He was not coming back.

Nick and I sat down and started some small talk with this group of strangers who turned out to be very friendly. The first person I sat beside was Hadas. I recognized her name as Israeli and soon learned that her parents were born in Israel. We exchanged some broken Hebrew and then got on to chatting about our weekends and eventually our lives. She told me about growing up in New York State before moving out to California for college. She had been in San Diego ever since. She had just moved in with her boyfriend of two years and was feeling excited and hopeful about this new adjustment. "I feel good about the decision," I remember her saying. "We both want it, but it feels a little bit too grown up for me, if you know what I mean?" she said. "Don't talk to me about growing up," I replied. "It's not my speciality."

Hadas gave me a funny look. "What do you do for work?" she asked. At this point I paused. I hate this question. I usually do everything to avoid asking or answering this question. I am always super-confident when speaking to people and look them in the eyes, but I find that when I tell them I am a lawyer I always look away and break eye contact. I am still not super-comfortable with it. "I'm a lawyer," I replied, awaiting the theatrics. She looked to my bare feet, long curly hair and generally unkempt appearance. Then she released a loud "Ha!" and broke out into laughter. "You – a lawyer. That wouldn't have been my first guess. But hey – you are way more grown up than me." I looked to the ground. "Well, that depends on what you do?" She unleashed a big smile and replied proudly: "I'm a yoga teacher and I run a stand-up paddle ('SUP') yoga business out of Encinitas, California." *How do I always find these people?* I thought to myself.

At this point in my life, Yoga Law was still an idea in my mind but I began barraging Hadas with questions. I was so incredibly impressed with her answers. It was clear that Hadas knew exactly what she was doing, except that she was missing the final pieces. She showed me her Instagram, which was stellar, and explained to me how she came up with her own SUP sequences that had a cult-like following in Southern California. For the next hour, all we did was talk about the industry and her goals, what she has accomplished, what she would like to accomplish and where she saw opportunity for growth with her business. I was enthralled.

"One day, I realized I didn't really have a life because I was teaching so much. I was making good money, sure, but I wanted my life back. Every week would end in sheer exhaustion. One night after I fell into bed completely worn out, I tossed and turned and tried to figure out how to clone myself. People loved my classes and the style of SUP I had created. But there was only one of me to execute. What could I do? I had lingered on this thought for almost two years, but I had taken no action. Ultimately, I realized nothing would change until I changed it. So, I did something a little bit crazy. I told the Universe I was going to run a teacher training and put up one post on my Instagram advertising a weekend certification in my style of SUP. I put registration at fifteen spots and was shocked in a week when all the spots were full and three people were on the waiting list." I could see that she was thinking things through, still a little unsure of her direction but also thrilled that the Universe had answered her call. "So, I'm going to run the teacher training and see what happens."

This was the absolute ideal scenario from my perspective, and Hadas was in a position that I work so hard to get all of my clients to reach. I had to quell my excitement. "That is amazing," I said. "So, you haven't run this teacher training just yet?" I asked. "Nope. We'll start it in two months." "And do you have copyright certificates and licensing agreements in place?" I asked. Hadas looked at me blankly, a gaze that I have become so familiar with when breaking the ice on legal talk. "Nope. Should I? Oh no, what am I forgetting?" she asked in a panic. "Don't worry," I told her, "we are going to sort you out. You are in an awesome position to crush it and I am so excited for you."

Just as I finished this sentence, I felt Jesse shove me from behind. "Come on dude, we are going," he said. I did not even know how much time had passed, having been so present in the conversation. I got Hadas' number and we agreed to chat on the phone. It was likely that I would not be able to act as her lawyer because I did not know the nuances of American IP law, but I did want to point her in the right direction and help out. It would also serve as a great learning opportunity for me to see what works and how I could help get my clients into a position similar to Hadas'. *"Nayeem mayod,"* she said in Hebrew, which means "nice to meet you." "Hadas, YES!" was all I said, backing away. I bid her friends adieu and ran to catch up with Jesse and Nick.

I set up a time to chat with Hadas the next Monday and was giddy with excitement as the phone rang. From the moment she picked up and said *"Shalom,"* it was like our conversation from the beach had never ended. I told her that I was happy to volunteer my time to help her and make her process of professionalization easy. On my end, this was my first time working with a client who was truly expanding into the licensing and growth phase of their business. I was eager to learn.

I explained to Hadas that the first thing she should do is register her teaching manual with the United States Copyright Office. While the copyright in a work arises when the work is created, registering for copyright adds additional protection, clearly outlines a copyrighted work (which is ideal for a licensing agreement) and only costs $35 to complete. Before handing her SUP Teaching Manual over to her students, Hadas would have a copyright certificate to protect her IP in her creation.

The next step for Hadas was to work on a licensing agreement. In this agreement, we would clearly set out the IP that her business owned. She had successfully registered a trademark and now had this copyright certificate for the teaching manual. I worked with Hadas to develop an agreement that would allow her to share this IP with students in her teacher training without the risk of losing any of it. We made sure to include the following key terms that were important to her: The license was revocable (she could withdraw it if certain rules were broken); use of the manual did not amount to a transfer of ownership; the license was granted for a term of three years, and then it would need to be renewed for a cost; and any use of the materials had to follow strict rules, all of which would benefit Hadas' business.

This is where the licensing agreement got super juicy. We put in provisions that said if anyone was going to teach the licensed materials, they would need to reference Hadas' business as the source. For example, anytime someone taught a SUP class in accordance with what they had learned in the teacher training, they would need to promote the class by referencing Hadas' Instagram account and including a link to her website.

In hindsight, these promotional provisions were really key to Hadas' business growth. And boy did she grow.

Just one short year later, Hadas was busy travelling the globe, leading master teacher trainings and running retreats all over the world. We worked together in drafting licensing agreements for each new teacher training that she operated. Before we knew it, Hadas had an army of different SUP yoga teachers around the world, all promoting her brand and all enjoying life passionately. I was so proud of Hadas and had learned a lot from working with her.

It just so happened that I was travelling in Israel in late 2017 and looked up different activities to do while I was staying in Tel Aviv. Well, wouldn't you know it? Hadas was running SUP yoga classes just outside of Gordon Beach. I saw her schedule online and popped into a class to surprise her. *"Shalom Achoti"* (meaning "hello, my sister") I said with a big smile as she and I made eye contact. I hugged her boyfriend Eli, whom I had come to know quite well over time. It looked like Hadas was wiping a tear from her eye as we laughed about her success and her current dream life. "I never, ever thought I would cry when seeing my lawyer," she joked with a few giggles. Turning serious, she said, "Okay, grab your board and let's practice in the water."

I picked up the heavy board and walked toward the Mediterranean Sea with Modest Mouse's "Float On" playing in my head. IP never seemed so cool.

Your Chapter Checklist:

The FUN key points about protecting and building your brand:
- Reverse Engineering your business means thinking about the life you want, how/where you want to live it

and how you can build your business to accommodate and fuel that lifestyle.

- IP laws exist to protect people's unique creations, legally creating the freedom to be the exclusive owner of any such creations and also preventing anyone from copying their creations.

- Trademarking protects a logo, word or series of words which allows you the exclusive use of the trademark for specific goods and services.

- Copyright protects artistic creations and at law, someone has copyright once they create something without the need to formally register the copyright (although it can be a good idea to do so).

- You can license your materials for others to use for a cost (or for free) which will dictate the rules around how they can use your IP. However, you can only license what you legally own, so taking steps to organize your IP in order to license it in the future can be an excellent idea.

Chapter 8

Operating Online

Intention

The year is 2019 and it is almost inevitable that your yoga business is operating online – and if it is not, then it likely soon will be. If you have a business, you have a website. If you have a website, there are rules you need to follow to be at best legal practices. In the most FUN way possible, this chapter will outline the rules that yoga professionals must follow when operating online, which extend to privacy policies, terms and conditions, and disclaimers.

If you remember only one thing from this chapter, remember to think of your website and online operations as a store that your customers come to visit. Just as there are rules you have to follow when you own and operate a store, there are rules you need to follow when operating online. If you can keep this big-picture perspective in your head, it will be easier to understand why these rules apply to you.

The Golden Rule Applies

As with every other aspect of law that we've discussed so far, the Golden Rule applies to operating online. And that rule is: Be a good person and communicate your expectations openly and honestly to all those you have relationships with. We need to apply this rule to privacy policies, terms and conditions for your website, and disclaimers.

The Golden Rule for privacy policies is very straightforward: Be crystal clear with people about what information you are collecting from them, why you are collecting that information, how you will use that information, whether any third party will receive that information, and how people can change the information that you've collected from them.

When it comes to terms and conditions for your website, the Golden Rule simply means being straight up with people about what they can expect when purchasing your services online and accessing your online services. Remember, there are no good terms to an agreement and there are no bad terms to an agreement, but only those that *reflect a relationship you seek to have*. People can choose to work with you on your terms, so long as you tell them upfront what to expect.

Finally, for a disclaimer, the Golden Rule means that you should explain your yoga qualifications, what you are trained to teach and what you are not qualified to share. When you are straight up with people about your qualifications and how they can – or can't – rely on information you share with them, they have the ability to choose whether or not to follow you. But if you aren't honest with people and mislead them about what qualifications you have, then you can get into a lot of trouble. The whole point of a disclaimer is that people who read it agree they do not hold you responsible for the consequences of following what you tell them, so it is best to do this when they know exactly what qualifications you have in leading/guiding them online.

What's the Deal With... Privacy Policies?

A privacy policy outlines how a business/website/person collects, uses and discloses personal information that they receive about people. You may be wondering why you need a privacy policy. Governments across the world are going to great lengths to protect online consumers and users, giving them the right to find out how websites track their behaviour and what personal information a website will keep, collect and possibly sell. Simply put, that is what all of this is about. It has never been more important to have an effective privacy policy, because the collection of people's personal information online has never been a more relevant topic. We only have to look at news stories about how global elections are seemingly influenced by the plethora of personal information that websites collect from their users.

There are a handful of different laws from around the globe that outline specific needs and requirements for privacy policies. Reading them all is an excellent way to take a nap. I feel it would be more effective to explain how privacy works at the macro level to make sure that you understand the general concepts, instead of getting lost in the incredibly mundane specifics of the laws. Like all areas of law that I discuss in this book, I think that being aware of the relevant relationships will empower you to act responsibly and reasonably within them.

In short, I feel it would be best for you to understand the overarching principles around privacy laws and operating online, so that you can be empowered to understand what this is about and why it matters. You will understand what needs to be included in your privacy policy, generally speaking, and where you can go for further resources.

It Doesn't Matter Where You Operate – It Matters Who Gives You Their Information

The Internet is incorporeal and spans across all countries and continents of the world. Usually, the specific laws that apply to you will be in the jurisdiction where you live. For example, if you operate a business in Colorado and own a yoga studio in Steamboat Springs, Colorado, most of the laws that apply to you will be municipal (town or city) or state laws, with some federal laws applying as well. In this regard, it is easy for you to play by the rules, because you know where you operate and what you have to do to be at best legal practices in your particular area.

However, when you operate a business online and collect people's personal information, things become a bit trickier. This is because many of the rules pertaining to privacy policies are determined by the jurisdiction of the people who are sharing their information with you, not the jurisdiction where you are based. For example, let's say that you are based in Cochrane, Alberta and have an awesome online handstand workshop that you sell on your website. You have a monthly newsletter with thousands of subscribers from all over the world and sell products through Shopify. In operating this business and collecting their personal information (at a minimum, you have their email address because they are on your mailing list), you are bound to abide by the privacy laws of their jurisdiction, in addition to the jurisdiction where you operate.

This may seem overwhelming. How can you keep abreast of all privacy laws for all jurisdictions at one time? The good news is that lawyers are here to help you. And if you don't want to work with a lawyer, you can follow the information below to make sure that you cover *most* of what is needed for these policies. As e-commerce continues to grow, the world of privacy policies changes as more and more legislation (specifically in California) continues to emerge, and one must remain mindful of what is required to stay at best practices.

Since we are on the subject of California, the State of California has always been a pioneer in consumer protection and that is no different when it comes to privacy policies. Most of California's privacy legislation (for example the "Shine the Light" law and the *California Consumer Privacy Act of 2018)* offers rules that heavily favour consumers. The reason this matters to you is because these laws apply to consumers in California and not businesses operating out of California.

We are talking about the yoga industry here, so there will likely be at least one person from California whose personal information you hold (I hope that joke landed). The good news is that the California Consumer Privacy Act of 2018 pertains to businesses that make over $25 million in annual revenue or that make over half of their money from selling personal information. You likely do not check off either of these boxes, but if you do, be sure to consult with a lawyer to make sure that your privacy policy is up to date.

Privacy Policies: The Specifics and How to Use Them

Remember what all of this is about: You are collecting people's information online and there are certain rules you have to follow in how you collect the information and what you do with it. Most of the things you should address in your privacy policy are as follows:

- What information you will collect from people (name, email, birthday, credit card info).

- How you will use the information you collect via your website.
- How you will develop and implement policies to protect personal information.
- Who will be available to address questions/concerns/complaints from the public.
- Why you collect the information that you are collecting.
- How you have clearly obtained consent from the people submitting their information.
- Whether you will only use the information for the purposes you are collecting it.
- Whether the information you collect is necessary to achieve the purposes for which you are requesting it.
- How people have the option to opt out of marketing campaigns (usually achieved with an "unsubscribe" button in your emails/newsletters).
- Whether you share personal information with third parties, and if so, which third parties and for what purposes. If you share the information with third parties for marketing purposes, you must ensure that the person whose information you hold has a chance to withdraw their consent.
- How you will store the information and how you will destroy it.
- How you will keep information up-to-date and accurate.
- Explain how you will protect the information from theft or cyber theft (passwords being a good method).
- Whether you use cookies, and if so, how you use them (see below under "Cookies").
- What simple process you offer for people to access the information you hold about them.

- What simple system you have created to address and respond to any complaints.
- What date your privacy policy became effective.

The best way to address the above points is to have a privacy policy on your website, often not a page of its own on the main website but noticeable as a footer. Once people click the link labeled *Privacy* or *Privacy Policy* at the footer of your website, they should be directed to a separate page that has all of the information listed above under *Privacy Policy: The Specifics*. If you include all of that information, you will be circumventing 99.9 percent of any potential issues that could come your way regarding your privacy policy and how you hold the personal information of others.

Cookies

I don't get angry often, but I am upset with the person who first called this particular type of Internet procedure *cookies*. I'll never forget the first time I got an email from a client with the subject "Cookies" and felt elated. One of my clients had cookies for me because they loved me so much for being a great lawyer! When I opened the email I was slightly deflated to see a question about the client using cookies on their website. That was the last time I ever got excited seeing the word cookies.

Cookies is a term used to describe a process in which the websites you browse (or third parties) drop a file on your computer that is stored there to track your online activities. This is a sneaky move because it gives marketers and other companies a chance to track your online behaviour. The good news is that you can always delete cookies from your browser. But obviously cookies can be an invasion of your privacy. As such, the rules are changing now so that websites meeting a certain threshold have to notify you that they use cookies before you even use the website. As a best practice measure, I tell clients that if they can organize it through WordPress or Squarespace or the likes to have a "cookie" prompt come up, do it! If their website does not offer this, I always encourage them to include a provision in their privacy policy that clearly communicates whether or not they use cookies.

Terms and Conditions: What Are They and What Do They Include?

I want you to think about the terms and conditions of your website as the rules that you make with people for how they should use your website and make purchases from your website. Terms and conditions are called many different things, like for example *Terms of Service*, but on a practical level just think about them as a means of communicating what people can expect from visiting your website or buying your goods online.

As I mentioned before, the year is 2019. While the world used to work in a way where people would physically walk into a store, nowadays almost everything happens by people visiting you online. Your website and social media are your store, your business card and your mouthpiece all combined into one. Since your website does all the talking for you, you have to make sure it is saying all of the right things to protect you and ensure that you are participating in relationships how you would like to.

There isn't a specific prescription for what should be included in the terms and conditions you post on your website. Just like there isn't a "good" contract, there aren't "good" terms and conditions. What matters most is that you are comfortable with what you communicate to the people who visit your "online store" and to the people who will take the information you share to heart. With this being said, here are some of the common items you'll find in terms and conditions or terms of service:

- *Copyright* – a statement explaining that even if you do not have the registered copyright sign by your works, you still assert and maintain all copyright in your works.

- *Purpose* – an explanation of why you put information on your website, so that you do not confuse people (i.e. "I share information about crow pose and other yoga poses because it is fun and I love sharing information that I learned on my own" vs. "I am a certified yoga teacher and I instruct students how to properly do poses").

- *Links to third-party websites* – a disclaimer about any links you post to third-party websites, stating that you are not responsible for anything that the third-party website does. This is an important "CYB" (cover yo' butt) provision.

- *License to use materials* – a statement explaining that people who use your website are granted a temporary (not permanent) and revocable (you can retract it, if you want) license to materials on the website, such as any blogs or free downloads. The statement can also set conditions for using materials on your website, like for example a condition that the material cannot be sold to any third party.

- *Limitation of liability and disclaimers* – a provision explaining that you have no liability for anything that may arise from someone using your website. In plain English, "use at your own risk." Disclaimers are a great place to state your qualifications and what you are not qualified for, and let people know that they are solely responsible for following the information posted on your website (see below under "Disclaimers").

- *No Guarantees* – if desired, a statement letting people know that there are no guarantees to any content on your website (i.e. "Lost that last five pounds with a savasana-only exercise").

Disclaimers

In my opinion, it is very important to include disclaimers as part of the terms and conditions of your website, even though you may not be 100 percent obligated to do so. I say this because generally speaking, disclaimers do a very good job of setting the appropriate expectations for someone using your website or following information on it.

In a disclaimer you are telling people that *they are entirely responsible* for any actions they take or do not take based on the content on your website. You can state that you are putting the information on your website strictly for educational purposes and do not guarantee any results from what people do with the information. People can follow what you are saying if they want, but they certainly don't have to. Further, you can let people know your exact qualifications so that there can be no confusion about who you are or any claim that you've misled them.

The formula is simple:

1. You explain who you are, where you've studied, what your qualifications are (i.e. a 200-hour certified yoga teacher) and also what you are not (i.e. a medical professional, a registered nutritionist), so that people can be totally clear about who they are listening to and

can decide on their own how much weight to put into what you are sharing with them.

2. You let readers/viewers know that they are fully responsible for anything they choose to do based on the information you include on your website.

3. You let them know there are no guaranteed results from them working with you or using your services or following tips you may share with them.

4. You make it an obligatory condition of using your website that readers fully release you from liability for anything that may arise from them reading or applying information you publish on your website. This is a *critical* part of your terms and conditions.

5. You tell readers to contact you if they are unsure or have any questions. (Note: I recommend this to clients because it is a sensible thing to do, and if nothing else it would show an objective third party [a mediator, arbitrator, judge] that you acted reasonably.)

Lessons Learned from Taking a Business Online: Conscious Counsel

Taking my legal practice, Conscious Counsel, online is one of the best decisions I have ever made. With no previous experience in doing anything online except writing emails and watching YouTube videos, I really didn't know what I was doing. But in line with sentiments previously expressed in this book, *I knew that if I wanted to travel and work at the same time badly enough, then I would make it work.* Now, just over fourteen months since first "taking the plunge" online, I have learned so much and am happy to share some basic tips and tricks that would have helped me immensely if only someone had shared them with me before I started.

Reverse Engineering

The most important thing when building a business online is understanding with absolute clarity exactly what you will and will not be offering in terms of goods and services. Obviously, you'll want to ensure that you are selling things that you'll be able to offer online. So for example, as a yoga teacher, it wouldn't make sense to build an online yoga teacher training course and also offer one-to-one instruction, unless your clients are willing to do so online. While this seems like a very simple step, you just want to be extremely clear (both for yourself and your clients) about what exactly you offer, so that you can ensure you offer all of it professionally and with integrity from anywhere around the world.

Set Expectations for Yourself

When I took my business online, I thought that it would mean I would work a lot less, which in hindsight is likely the opposite of the truth. Honestly, I work all the time, except I do so at very strange times and often in spurts. When you work online, you still work as hard as anyone who sits in an office at a desk all day – the difference (and the beauty of it all) is that you get to work on your own time schedule. This can be tricky if you are not determined or disciplined enough to work when you need to. (Note: Revisit the *why* of running your own yoga business if you need any motivation.) But over time, you can learn to work smart and that is the best. As you begin, you must set the expectation that you will have to work hard and smart (not always a lot) and that you won't mind because you'll love your work.

. The other expectation you need to have for yourself is patience. I've worked with hundreds of clients who run small businesses, and I've seen some succeed and I've seen some fail. I've usually been able to predict who will make it and who won't, but of course I always keep this to myself. I think the two most significant characteristics that determine whether a business will fail are: 1) Hastiness, or the need to succeed *immediately*; and 2) the need to make money immediately, which usually leads to decisions that are made mostly around financials instead of the values and integrity of the business.

From this gleaning, the only expectations that I would implore you to incorporate into your yoga business are self-love, patience and trust. Love yourself and be proud of yourself for your wins and losses (losses are also called opportunities). Be patient because things take time (I had the idea for this book three years ago, wrote most of it one year ago, and I am only finishing it at the start of 2019). And, trust that everything happens as it should. Always expect these things from yourself – you deserve it!

Set Expectations with Your Clients and Your Team

There are two other branches for setting expectations when you build an online business. The first is setting expectations with your clients, and the second is setting expectations with your team.

In terms of setting expectations with your clients, you are going to want to be totally transparent about how often you will be available to clients and in what capacities. Depending on the capacity in which you are operating an online yoga business – for example, teacher training, workshops, coaching other teachers, or leading one-to-one practices – your clients are going to want your attention and guidance. Because they don't get to see you in person and are always online, it is much easier for them to text you, email you or send you a direct message on Instagram. Before you begin working with your clients, it is best to let them know your availability (which you get to decide) and what they can expect from you in working together.

As a lawyer, it took a bit of courage for me to tell clients that they could not reach me whenever they wanted (as is expected in the legal industry), and that instead they would have to use a schedule that worked for us both. In my experience, no one minded at all because I told them upfront and let them know they had the option to work with someone else if they wanted. Well, some were looking for a lawyer they could call at any hour and some didn't really care. The key is that I told them what to expect at the beginning, so it was possible to have great working situations afterwards. There have been many instances when my clients were in a jam and I have fielded calls in the middle of the night or woken up super early to get something done. But that is my choice because I love my clients. And when you love someone, you'll do anything to make sure they are okay.

Finally, you need to set expectations with your team. Please do pay attention to these words. I hope you will be able to learn from my lessons. The biggest mistake I made when taking my business online was not making sure that the decision was cool with my team. I went from being based in Vancouver/Muskoka and then suddenly deciding overnight that I would be gone for eight months. I didn't consider the effect this would have on my team, who were highly motivated to be working with me because they liked being around me. Unfortunately, I lost members of my team due to this decision. Now I am very clear in communicating how I will work with my team online.

I have learned two important lessons from this experience:

1. Always tell people exactly how you intend your relationship to be. Before I work with anyone now, I'll have at least two Zoom or phone meetings in which I say that there is a very good chance we'll never meet in person. We'll have weekly meetings, chat on Slack, but if they are looking for a friend – I'm not it. This shift has helped me tremendously in finding and working with the right team (shout out to Cecilia and Simona for being the most incredible people to work with remotely!).

2. Be aware of why and how people want your energy from you. When people insist on spending time together or having my time in person, I am always aware of it. Of course, every person needs something different from a relationship. I have just gotten to a place where I'm very selective about who I spend my time with in person, including the people I work with. If someone needs to be close to you or always with you, this could be a red flag for a healthy working relationship, unless of course it is what you are both looking for.

Your Chapter Checklist:

Here we go. The big takeaways from operating online:

- If you are operating online, you will need to follow the rules and have a Privacy Policy, Terms and Conditions and a Disclaimer. These protect you from all the people who visit your site and use your content, without you even knowing it.

- Privacy Policies let people know what information you collect from them and how you use it. People have a right to know before sharing their personal information with you.
- The Terms and Conditions for your website and services will let people know what they can expect from accessing your information and using your services. Communicate this as clearly as possible from the start to avoid future headaches.
- Disclaimers are really important in protecting you from those you access and use your information. You tell people your qualifications and what they can expect from working with you or the information you provide (i.e. you don't promise they will be able to touch their toes). Ultimately, they agree not to hold you responsible for anything that happens to them based on them following your information or guidance.

Chapter 9

Putting It All Together: Yoga Festival

Intention

This chapter will illustrate the complexities of the relationships involved in organizing and executing a full-scale yoga festival. The issues that arise when organizing a big yoga event, like a festival, touch upon all the areas of the law that I have covered in this book. The Muskoka Yoga Festival story is an excellent example of what issues yoga professionals will come up against when they pursue and build their dream community events. Also, if you are curious how to do something like build a yoga festival, this chapter should be helpful.

If you remember only one thing from this chapter, remember to get all of your relationships down in writing. Communicate the expectations of your relationships as clearly as you possibly can, and try to anticipate as many unpredictable outcomes as possible so that you can work your way through them.

Dedication

This chapter is dedicated to Ashley Boone, without whom there would never have been a Muskoka Yoga Festival. I would also like to thank everyone who ever worked to bring Muskoka Yoga Festival to life, in its first, second and now third year.

How to Read This Chapter

When reading his chapter, all I want you to do is become aware of all of the relationships that a person or entity will have when putting on a major event, and then see how those relationships connect back to what you have already read in this book. Remember, law is just the structure around all the different relationships we have. We agree to work with someone, to buy something from someone, to sell something to someone, to receive sponsorship money from someone – and we memorialize our expectations around that relationship. Who will give what to whom at what time for how much. One of the biggest challenges in organizing a festival is the sheer volume of relationships you'll have at any given time.

There are three important things to mention before the story begins.

The first thing is that while this chapter deals with a festival, the legal implications and general lessons can be applied to almost any yoga event – or now that I think of it, any event at all. I have worked with five or six clients who organize yoga festivals, so I know how it works pretty well. But if you want to do a one-day yoga-thon or SUP yoga full moon party, or whatever you think would be amazing, these lessons still apply. At any time during reading, feel free to substitute the words *yoga festival* for whatever event you are thinking of creating and apply the lessons accordingly.

Secondly, the *critical* thing for you to remember in this chapter (and this book) is that anything is possible. I was able to witness, first-hand, how a dream turned into reality. Literally, a group of people who had a combined experience of zero in putting on a yoga festival were able to join forces and make something magical happen. The event was special but we were all ordinary yet driven and dedicated people who made it happen. If we could do it, so can you! My intention is that you see how anyone can create anything, without any experience, if they work hard enough to do it.

Lastly, as I tell this story, I am going to share some insights and lessons that I have learned from organizing two yoga festivals. Having gone through the experience, I know how much I would have benefitted from having someone share important tips and tricks with me, which makes me even happier to pass them forward.

The First Step: It Starts with an Idea

I met Ashley Boone while attending the Banff Yoga Festival in Banff, Alberta. I had driven to Banff with one of my best mates, Paul Gelinas (who would go on to found the Vancouver Acro Yoga Festival), and had been working with the Banff Yoga Festival organizers to set them up with some documents for the festival. The event was wonderful and we had a really special time. During my time there, I reflected on how much I enjoyed festivals for bringing people together and introducing me to new and amazing people.

I bumped into Ashley randomly, as two people do at an outdoor event. She was walking with a friend and there was too much space around us not to say hi. I was immediately struck by her strong presence and radiant smile. We did an awesome job of having a pretty lame, typically Canadian, friendly surface-level conversation until she said that she owned a yoga studio in Bracebridge, Ontario. My ears perked, just like a pup who hears a car pull into the driveway.

"My folks have a cottage in Bracebridge," I said. She gave me the glare that only locals can give cottagers before politely continuing, "…How amazing is Muskoka?" And then we spoke about Muskoka at great length, how it was our favourite place in Canada and how much we truly loved it. "I wanna put on a yoga festival in Muskoka," she said. And my eyes twinkled. I could just see it: Yoga mats on the grass, by the river, amongst the trees, with the sun setting on the horizon. It had to be.

I was, in fact, so moved by these fantasies created by Ashley that I decided to wait a whole six months before even remembering Ashley and the idea for a yoga festival in Muskoka. I had come back to Ontario to visit my family in late August and remembered that person I randomly met in Banff. We connected and hung out at Kirby Beach right on Lake Muskoka, dipping our toes in the water and dreaming big. We revisited the topic of a festival and this time with more vigour. Without seeing or doing a tour of Annie Williams Memorial Park (the venue), we figured it would be the best venue in Bracebridge for our event. I told Ashley to reserve it for a weekend in summer 2017. She called me the next day to let me know that it was in fact available and a $1500 deposit was required to reserve the space. The weekend of July 8–9 was the only remaining slot in the park's schedule and we needed to decide quickly.

Ashley came by my parents' cottage. The first moments of our hangout were a bit tense, each of us feeling the other out as to how serious we were about doing this. I had to pause for a moment when speaking to Ashley, readjust my eyes because it suddenly hit me that I really didn't know who this person was. I'd met her twice and now I was on the verge of committing to a massive project together. I was on the verge of starting my own law firm and wasn't really looking for an additional undertaking. But something about this felt right, even though it was so amorphous. I knew one thing for sure – my life had been shaped infinitely for the better because of yoga festivals, and if I could create something that might make another person's life better then it would all be worth it.

I looked at Ashley, zoning back into our conversation. There looked to be a small, bright twinkle in her eye. We held eye contact for a moment. I smiled. She smiled. "Let's just go for it and see what happens," she said. I jumped up for joy. We were going to create a yoga festival!

It is at this juncture that everyone can relate to this story. Haven't you had so many cool ideas you just never really acted upon? In my life, the Muskoka Yoga Festival was officially idea #2,466 that I had. Up to this point, none of the ideas really left the ground, usually because I came up with an idea on my own or decided to work on it with friends. When working alone, I found it too easy to quit or I didn't care enough about what I was doing to see it all the way through. In hindsight, almost all of my previous ideas were somehow related to me or my success, and in the absence of a greater purpose I was never compelled enough to see them through. When working with friends or family, our relationship was always friends first, or family always, and so there was less accountability to see it through. The point I am seeking to illustrate is that, for whatever reason, it wasn't until I started a project with a complete stranger that I was really able raise my accountability and commitment levels.

The Second Step: Why Am I Doing This?

The *first* step to putting on a yoga festival is having an idea. Done. Easy. But the second step was figuring out why we were putting on a yoga festival and *how* this yoga festival would be different from other festivals. Holding coffee mugs in our hands as we dipped our toes in the lake, we began to think about what the Mission, Vision and Values of our yoga festival would be. Intuitively, simply by being surrounded by giant trees, a vast lake and the clear blue sky, we knew that nature had to play a really big role in putting on this event. And the more we discussed how much we loved Muskoka – its rivers, forests and endless vistas, each one more beautiful than the next – it was clear why we wanted to do this here. We wanted to bring people out into nature so that they could experience this very special part of the world. Better yet, we wanted to use yoga and a positively intentioned community gathering as the vehicle to give people the excuse to come out here. Spending time outdoors had been second nature to Ashley and me for our whole lives. We wanted to give people who usually spend time in the city, or have little exposure to nature, the time and space to enjoy the outdoors and its incredible gifts.

Ashley had spent most of her life living in Bracebridge and cared for the town with all of her heart. She vehemently wanted to raise the vibrations of yoga in this special part of Canada and was looking to leave her mark. Having been a yoga studio owner for five-plus years, yoga was her second nature. It was what she knew best. The combination of Bracebridge and yoga seemed predestined. Personally, I loved the idea because I recognized how fortunate I was to spend part of my life in such a beautiful place like Muskoka. I would travel the world and tell people about Lake Muskoka and how it had to be the best place in the entire world. As my circle of friends in Toronto grew, I noticed that none of my new friends had spent any time in Muskoka. They would look at me puzzled: Heaven on earth was only ninety minutes away, but they hadn't been. I was determined to share it with them. And although I only practiced yoga and was not yet a teacher, most of the defining formative experiences in the past three years of my life had taken place at yoga festivals. So I wanted to contribute.

We knew that this entire party was going to be about doing yoga in nature. But, so what? Anyone can plan to do any sort of gathering in nature. The more we spoke about it, the more we realized that we had a special opportunity to do something that no one else in the world could do – put on a yoga festival in Muskoka. *This was a critical moment in understanding who we were.* It was obvious to us that there may be thousands of other yoga festivals in the world and there may be thousands of other events in Muskoka, but there was no yoga festival in Muskoka. We were courageously (and ignorantly) unafraid of any competing festivals because whatever they were, they weren't in Muskoka. There was only one Muskoka Yoga Festival (MYF) and it was ours.

Once we realized this, it immediately became apparent that it was our *obligation* to make MYF as Muskoka as possible. I'm not sure if you've read the book *Good to Great* by Jim Collins, but if you haven't, go buy it today. It is a brilliant composition of information coupled with clever themes about why successful companies succeed. In the book, he has something he calls "The Hedgehog Principle" that basically states the following: Whatever you are going to do, make sure you can be the best in the world at it. Accidentally, Ashley and I landed upon our hedgehog and decided to put all of our energy into the one thing that we were doing and no one else was – a yoga festival in Muskoka.

After landing on what made us different and why, the ideation of the festival came a lot easier. We drafted a mission statement that revolved around building a community of nature-loving, tree-hugging, downward-dog-doing human beings in Muskoka. We created a vision that would facilitate experiences for people to check out of the city and check in with themselves, making new friends and wonderful memories along the way.

When it came to our values, I'm proud to say that we really hit it on the head: Community, Connection and Conservation. Our goal was to build a community of positive, friendly people who appreciate nature and enjoy practicing yoga – not just asanas, but yogic lifestyle. We wanted to have people connect with themselves, with each other and with nature. And we wanted all of our efforts to showcase conservation of the environment. We agreed that each year we would partner with some form of social action organization that focused its efforts on protecting natural habitats. In the first year, we aptly chose the Muskoka Conservancy. Our profits would be shared with this organization and we would use the event to bring its incredible efforts and programs to a larger audience. The most important aspect of having these values is that they served as a reference point for almost every decision we made in organizing MYF. If a tough decision was needed, we'd talk about it and ask, "Does this connect to Community, Connection or Conservation?" and then the answer about what to do would reveal itself.

Now we were in good shape. We knew who we were, why we were doing what we were doing, and how we were going to go about doing it. All we needed to do was... do it.

The first step that we had to take care of was securing the venue. We liaised with the town of Bracebridge and were confirmed for July 8–9, 2017 at Annie Williams Memorial Park. Next, we knew that we had to buy a website domain and luckily www.muskokayogafestival.com was available. We hired a graphic designer to come up with the look and feel of the festival. We had a logo drawn up, built a Facebook page and put up a very basic website, with pictures supplied by Ashley of her doing yoga outdoors in Muskoka.

Here, it is worth mentioning the unique challenges of putting on an event for the first time. We hadn't done anything yet and everything we were planning to do was roughly ten months away. Our challenge was finding ways to communicate who we were and what we were about without having any content. It was here that I truly learned the power of branding. Through your words, images and arrangements, you can find ways to connect with people so that they understand exactly who you are.

For MYF, I always said that the festival was a whole bunch of air until the actual morning of the event began. It was all air. It was the air that our team would breathe into the event; it was the air that we would use to convert a dream into reality. It was the air we would manifest in our meditations. The first year was all about air. Most importantly, though, it taught me (and hopefully illustrates to you) the *power of creating with words*. I would take meetings or talk to volunteers or meet with sponsors and speak about the festival. In February, I could describe in the most specific details how the grass of the park smelled as people sat quietly in meditation. I could describe the setting sun over the venue as the band hit the stage and people began moving their body to dance. And of course, none of this existed. Yet. I had heard an expression somewhere about breathing reality into existence and now I realized how true that really was. *So, whatever it is you want to create or invent or facilitate, start talking about it now.* This is a critical step to making big things happen.

Legal Issue 1: Partnership or Incorporation

Legally, Ashley and I had a few important decisions to make. I'll elaborate on these so that you can understand our train of thought. The first question to answer was whether or not we would incorporate. In Chapter 4, Choosing Your Posture, we went into detail about incorporation and its legal repercussions. Here, we had to consider various factors in deciding whether or not to operate the Festival as a separate legal entity.

Obviously, we couldn't register the business as a sole proprietorship because there were two people who would own the business together. That was out of the question. We also knew that because we wanted to operate as a for-profit company, registering a society or a charity wouldn't make sense. So the only issue we really had to consider was whether we would form a partnership or register a company.

While there are benefits to registering and operating a partnership, there are risks that revolve around the fact that in a partnership, *partners share liabilities for the business and they share them personally.* This means that both partners share all debts owed by the business, and if one partner can't pay their share... well, then the responsibility is on the other partner to cover the tab. I knew that the festival would create a vast number of relationships and that we would be legally exposed in all of them. Since we had never done this before and didn't understand what we were doing, slipping up was not totally outside my reasonable set of expectations. In the event that we did mess up and were liable, I wouldn't want any personal assets to be at risk.

In addition to this, I had known Ashley for less than a month and didn't know anything about her past – if she was in debt, if she had any assets or if she'd been in any insolvent partnerships before. What I did know is that we were undertaking a fairly risky venture, basically incurring lots of costs to secure a venue, teachers and equipment for a big festival that we hoped people would show up for. They say in the festival business: If one breaks even their first year then they are very lucky. So, debt seemed inevitable. Adding all of these variables together – not knowing how much money Ashley had and the fact we were likely to incur some debt – I decided that it would be best to avoid a partnership. As such, we decided to incorporate.

Incorporating a company under these circumstances had its benefits. While we weren't thinking of tax repercussions just yet, we knew that if MYF was a total bust and we lost a whole ton of money on it, we wouldn't be personally responsible to pay the money back. This was a big factor. Furthermore, we also knew that holding a big yoga party for hundreds of people in the park is a fairly risky endeavour in terms of liability. While it would be fruitless to write out all the things that *could go wrong*, suffice it to say that the chances of an accident were not totally improbable. The benefit of being incorporated and having the company facilitate the event was that, again, all causes of action would be brought against the company and not us personally. If the company were to be sued and run out of money, its insolvency would mark the end of the story. Ashley and I would be safe. Of course, these are all scenarios we hoped would never unfold, but we were still obligated to be aware of them. *These are the reasons why we chose to incorporate.*

Legal Issue 2: Drafting a Shareholder Agreement

A shareholder agreement is basically a document that outlines how the owners of the company wish to run the company. It sets out the rules of how the owners can behave when they have to make the easy and difficult decisions about running the company. For example, under what circumstances can new owners be brought on? Are the shares allotted at one time or do they vest over time to ensure that people stay engaged in the business?

One of the first projects I embarked upon after starting Conscious Counsel was to create a "Shareholders' Conversation Starter," which posed a bunch of questions for business owners to consider when drafting a shareholder agreement. It described scenarios that commonly arise between shareholders (which clients were unfamiliar with) and asked them how they would like the scenarios to be handled. For example, what happens if a third party wants to buy the business? An amazing offer is made and one person wants to sell for the cash but the other wants to continue building the business. Ashley and I needed to discuss these issues to ensure that we were on the same page. We learned a lot about each other during this time, including why we wanted to run this business and where we wanted to take it. It was reassuring to know that we were both committed to building it for the long term and wanted to establish deep roots for a yoga community in Muskoka.

It is worth adding that not signing a shareholder agreement is really easy because the document can be a bit confrontational. And when people first start a business, people love to believe that they are on the same page about everything and no one wants to ruffle any feathers. But if I've learned *anything* from my time working as a lawyer, I've learned that it is *better to have the difficult conversations at the start* instead of asking a lawyer to have them for you at the end. It is also a lot cheaper. In addition, there is nothing more frustrating than pouring over an agreement that is silent on the only issue you are really having. Don't ask me how or why but it always happens: A document has everything you need except the one issue you are fighting over.

Another issue with shareholder agreements is that they are often written in a way that people don't understand. Pages of legalese will flow but the people signing have no idea what they mean. This is almost worse than not having a document at all. Imagine signing away the rights to your business without even knowing what you have agreed to?! It never ceases to amaze me that people will invest so much time (every day of their life) and money (usually their savings) to start a business and then not set up its most crucial aspects in a way they can understand.

Ultimately, Ashley and I had a few discussions about what was important to us and had the document reflect our intentions. It was very tempting not to do this because we get along very well and trust each other, but it was important for it to be done. A simply drafted and plain-language shareholder agreement should come part and parcel of an incorporation to make sure that all ownership doubts or questions are properly taken care of.

Reflection: Not Having a Management Agreement

While Ashley and I were clear about our shared ownership of the company and the rules of how we would operate it as owners, we did lack a management agreement. Looking back, it would have been immensely beneficial to have one. A management agreement is a very simple document that outlines who will be responsible for what in their managerial roles. It divides the work of the company amongst the managers and clearly states – on paper – who will be responsible for doing what. This document is extremely important to have for communicative purposes, but also to provide a feeling of parity amongst the managers of a company.

For example, with a yoga festival, it would be helpful to determine who would be responsible for the following projects:

- Venue Organization
- Insurance
- Scheduling
- Teacher Selection
- Sponsorships/Grants
- Legal
- Vendors
- Volunteers
- Clothing/Apparel
- Security/Sanitation at Venue
- Finances/Accounting
- Ticket Sales
- Website
- PR/Marketing/Social Media

This is just a sample list of areas that should be addressed in a management agreement. Of course, the task should be done in a way that makes sense to the managers. The key thing with a management agreement is not that it becomes a legally binding agreement (although it can if you don't know/trust your fellow manager), but more so that it becomes an objective document you can review to ensure that everyone is pulling their weight.

In my experience with building a festival, I can tell you that we never had a clear management agreement and that is certainly a regret of mine. In hindsight, I can see some of the challenges that may prevent companies from having a management agreement: a) You have no idea what you are doing because you've never done it before, so at first you don't know what to include; b) you are so busy doing everything else that this just falls to the wayside; and c) you just never get around to it because you "know what you are doing," even though it is never clearly written anywhere.

Take my advice: *If you are working with another person or a group of people, write down your responsibilities. This will save you a lot of headaches and tension.* While Ashley and I were still able to do great work and do it respectfully while honouring each other, there was no question that it would have been much easier for us if we'd had a management agreement. Take the time, prioritize it and JUST DO IT.

Legal Issue 3: Two Trademark Stories

There is a whole chapter on intellectual property in this book (Chapter 7), so I will just briefly address our decision *not* to register *Muskoka Yoga Festival* as a trademark. I'd also like to share a story about another yoga festival's decision to trademark a particular mark before the festival took place and why that wasn't the smartest decision.

Basically, we were facing a very low risk that someone else would come up with the name *Muskoka Yoga Festival*, trademark it and then prevent us from using it moving forward. We knew this because we did the appropriate searches to see that the mark was unregistered. We scanned the web for hours and spoke with various municipal counsellors to learn that there was no other event with such a name or even a similar name. This mattered because we were going to be *the first people to use the mark for commercial purposes.* So, because we were the only ones using it, we knew that we had the best rights to its name and did not feel the need to incur the expense of registering the mark, especially with limited cash flow at the start, and especially because we didn't even know if all of this was going to happen.

But we could have been in trouble. For example, if another party were to register the trademark *Muskoka Yoga Festival* even without using it and only planning to use it in the future, they would have priority because they were registered and we were not. The trademark registry always rewards parties for taking the initiative to do things correctly. If that were to happen, we'd have to challenge the registration process and get roped into some legal work that would be expensive and take time. We would have to seek to have the registration rejected on the basis that we used it first. A whole not-fun process would unfold and then we'd need to focus our energy on that instead of building an awesome festival. Notwithstanding this, we still decided not to register *Muskoka Yoga Festival* as a trademark and I stand by that decision at the start.

The other story has to do with the trademark *"Canada's Yoga Festival."* This mark was registered by a festival called "Emerge" that was set to take place in July 2017 in Ontario, Canada, just outside of Ottawa – our nation's capital. Just like us, Emerge was a first-year festival and boasted a super impressive line-up of world-class teachers and musicians. Unfortunately, the festival had to cancel last minute due to a string of unforeseen events. This was a bummer for the whole community, as the jam would have no doubt been super special. Remember, all of this is about bringing people together to do great things and I'm sad that an event with such aspirations failed to come to fruition, both for the organizers and for the attendees.

Either way, I found it very peculiar that Emerge had trademarked the words *"Canada's Yoga Festival"* and plastered it on all of their posters and their website. I don't know who advised them to do this, but their decision to register a trademark before the festival had even happened was a bit strange. I was lucky to remember sage advice from an IP lawyer I had worked with in my earlier years of lawyering. I had jumped into his office to ask him a question about a trademark file, and he looked at me sternly and said: "You build a business first and then you register a trademark. You don't build a business off a trademark. Everyone thinks a clever slogan can bring them success overnight, but they are wrong. We always advise clients to build their business and then register their trademark. Not the other way around." I never fully grasped this concept until I saw what happened with Emerge.

It seemed to me that they thought there was this amazing mark, *"Canada's Yoga Festival,"* and that if they registered it they could build their business around it. But clearly, it didn't work because the festival never took place. They tried to build their business around their trademark, which was precisely what my mentor had told me businesses should not do. In best practices, a trademark should be a word, symbol, logo or phrase that the public uses to identify your product. But if your product doesn't exist yet, how can the public know about it? If you have a lot of cash and don't mind incurring the cost of registration, then it could make sense to register a mark at the same time you start your business, but you don't necessarily have to. I hope these illustrations shed some light on the decision to register a trademark and when it would be worthwhile to begin the process.

The Importance of Believing in Your Vision

If there is anything I learned from helping to put on an event like the Muskoka Yoga Festival, it is that you have to fully trust and believe that you will actually be able to do what you say you will do. The Universe will test you, it will throw a million problems your way, but ultimately you'll need to stand up to all the challenges and say, "We're still doing it and it's going to be amazing." This may be trite advice and I'm certainly not the first person to say it, but I can't stress how important it is. Your belief in the success of your festival or event will create that success.

Here is my favourite story from the Muskoka Yoga Festival to prove the point above. We'll fast forward to December 2016. At this point, Ashley and I had continued to work on the Festival, but we clearly had no idea what we were doing. We were in communication with a few teachers, had booked the venue, and had a Facebook page and a website. I had spoken with some contacts at different companies and received some really helpful advice about who might be the right people to connect with. I had meetings whenever I was in Toronto and tried to enrol as many people as possible for the Festival. But it was a first year festival taking place in July and no one was too interested to hear about it so early.

Despite this, Ashley and I wanted to put on a bit of an "MYF Welcome Event" in Toronto to gauge the interest of our community and brainstorm about what the Festival could be like. The awesome folks at lululemon were kind enough to lend us the attic space in their Queen Street store, and David Good, an awesome Toronto-based yoga teacher, agreed to teach. My best friend Evan volunteered to play beautiful acoustic guitar for the class. The idea was to have a class and then a discussion about what people would want in a festival. Things were shaping up! We posted on Instagram and Facebook a few weeks out that we'd be hosting this night and were stoked to dream big with our community. I sent out a bunch of invitations to my friends and Ashley did as well. Momentum was building and our first glimpse of how awesome MYF would be was just around the corner.

The big night came. My parents, who have supported me and loved me always, insisted on driving me down and attending the class. I've always appreciated and been grateful for how wonderful they have been. I was excited to show them what I'd been working on. The event was called for 7 p.m. and I arrived a bit early, waiting to welcome people. And then I waited. My best friend Josh showed with his dear fiancée at the time, Andi. Evan showed. David Good showed. Ashley's boyfriend at the time showed. My parents showed. And, that was really it. Two other people showed. I couldn't believe it; I was shocked. I had all these visions of epic hug circles and creative ideas and people being super excited for what we were planning. But, *only two people showed up* – and one of them I had to pull off the street. I have no idea how the other person heard about it. Part of me was gutted, but we still had fun. David taught a great class, Evan played beautifully and I was happy to be with my family and friends.

I prepared to leave with my folks and went to say goodbye to Ashley. We exchanged a glance that didn't need any explanation. I almost came to the words, "Should we still do this?" but didn't say anything. Ashley held a resolute smile and hugged me tightly. "Great job, my dear," she said cheerfully, and then she was off. I got into the backseat of my parents' car, feeling as if I had just been picked up from high school. My dad, a very smart business person and a very pragmatic person (not to mention my role model and best friend), looked at me in the rear-view mirror. "You sure you want to do this Cory?" he asked in a non-confrontational and supportive tone. I had a think about it and then responded. "Yes, of course. It is going to work." I didn't have a doubt. I still knew the concept made too much sense and was too fun not to work; we just needed to go about it in a different way.

In hindsight, this opportunity was the perfect out. If I had wanted to run away and be scared and embarrassed, I could have done that. I could have called Ashley, told her that I didn't think we could do it, that no one cared, that no one would show up and we'd be screwed. But I didn't. I realized this was a small failure and was really an opportunity to do things a lot smarter. We tried one thing that was a bust. Great. What's next? I'm glad that I stood up to the occasion and Ashley had the confidence to stick with our vision as well. This is where one of the benefits of a partnership comes in – if one person trips and stumbles, the other is there to pick them up. Ashley picked me up that night. She also carried me all the way to the end, but that is beside the point.

I feel fortunate to have learned some very important lessons early on. First and most importantly, I learned that no one really cares about what you are doing nearly as much as you do until you do it. It is sad but true. People just don't care and this shouldn't be taken personally. Everyone has their own life with their own priorities. Clearly, whatever you are doing is super important to you, but it isn't important to them – until you provide them with an amazing experience. Then they are interested. Secondly, I learned that if Ashley and I didn't believe that we'd be able to put on this festival, no one else would. During the *eureka* moment in my parents' car, I promised myself that my newest and most important role was going to be Festival Cheerleader. I was going to hype MYF as much as I could. Always. If there was even a miniscule element of doubt, it would all fall apart. And I never wavered. There were tense moments, but I always told everyone how incredible the Festival was going to be. We willed it into reality.

I share this story to let you know that failing can be awesome sometimes. Failing can teach you humbling lessons that you need to learn in order to be stronger and smarter. While you are allowed to fail, you are never allowed to not believe in what you are doing. You can lose everything except for that. I share this story at every MYF event we have just to share the importance of sticking with something even when it sucks. It is also a reminder that building a community takes time and patience. Savour each step of the journey and just know you'll be so proud to look back on how you overcame any doubters, always trusting supremely in yourself to succeed.

The Need for a Team

Shortly after the event at which two people showed up, I set off for a month in Africa and planned to start my trip by leading Yoga Law workshops with the Africa Yoga Project (AYP). I was connected to the organization through my incredible and supportive friend, not to mention wonderful human being, Christa Hull. Christa and I had met at a yoga festival and were buds ever since. She'd always had my back and done whatever she could to help me. It is guardian angel friends like Christa that inspire me to do whatever I can to help others. Christa had connected me with AYP's founder and Executive Director, Paige Elenson, who after a brief conversation on the phone invited me to stay at her place in Nairobi during my visit. I was surprised by the warm gesture and happily took her up on the offer.

I spent five days hanging out at the Africa Yoga Project headquarters and quickly became family with everyone there. After I ran my workshops, I helped out where I could and spent lots of time with the staff. We had a blast. We did spin classes together and I joined the AYP team for their Christmas party at a fun bar called K1 Klubhouse. I was lucky enough to participate in some of the yoga classes in the slums of Nairobi and chat with AYP teachers who were born in these communities. It was all together an incredibly inspiring and humbling time in my life, which showed me the incredible impact that yoga and heart-driven leaders can make in any part of the world.

However, what I relished most about the experiences was the chance to hang out with Paige in her home. She was a very busy person, but the candid conversations about her programs, vision and team set the wheels of my mind in motion. One constant theme she kept coming back to was the importance of her team and how her organization's vision for greater and deeper impact revolved around that team. It was clear to me that we needed to build a Muskoka Yoga Festival Team.

Upon returning to Vancouver after a very dreamy month-long African adventure, I spoke with Ashley and we agreed that we needed to build a team on the ground ASAP. Because Ashley was based in Muskoka and I was in British Columbia, it was clear that we needed someone who knew the Toronto scene, was well respected and had a genuine passion for cultivating guest experiences. We asked the Universe to send us this person and our prayers were answered on a cold February day. I received a text message from Ashley that read: "Just been in contact with a guy named Kurt on Facebook. Seems amazing. Contact him about being our Greater Toronto Area Lead."

I remember very clearly the first time I spoke to Kurt. I was with a bunch of guys from my football team, the Red Army, and we were planning to spend the afternoon watching sports at a pub. I called Kurt and spoke to him for thirty minutes about his life, what he was up to and any ideas he had about the Festival. I was pacing around outside Vancouver's Shark Club, trying to keep warm as Kurt and I kept talking and talking. I really liked this guy. During the conversation, I just kept laughing and smiling. I was having fun, on the phone! After I learned a bit about Kurt's experiences as a yoga professional, it was clear that he was the person we had been looking for. You ask and the Universe delivers. We had our first team member.

Things really picked up momentum after we brought Kurt on board. Suddenly, we were having meetings and throwing around names with some of the best instructors in Toronto and Muskoka. Ideas began flowing in new directions and a multitude of opportunities began to reveal themselves. While I loved hanging with Ashley, it was great to have someone else to talk to about the Festival. Kurt brought a great enthusiasm and incredible sense of humour to everything we were doing. We'd laugh and laugh and laugh. We'd laugh about meetings we had or ideas we had or random things we wanted to do with the Festival. It was as if a third paint brush had been added to our vision of the Muskoka Yoga Festival, someone who brought different colours, textures and shapes. Suddenly the picture we were painting was starting to take a different shape and form – and I liked it. As Kurt and I became better buddies, I realized that if it weren't for the Festival, we'd never have spent as much time together, and thus never gotten to know each other so well. But the more time we chilled, the more I grew fond of Kurt and appreciated his uniqueness. I immediately understood the importance of having a variety of opinions on board. And having gotten a taste of it, I wanted more.

In addition to knowing a lot of people who could teach at the Festival, Kurt also knew a lot of people in the Toronto yoga scene. When we came up with a list of the roles we were looking to fill for our team, Kurt recommended a few people to connect with. One of the first people was a guy named Drew. He was a yoga teacher around the city who was committed to building a career in yoga. He was intelligent, driven and had lots of ideas about partnerships for the Festival. I had a wonderful phone call with Drew from Café Musette in Vancouver. We hit it off right away and instantaneously established a connection. I loved this guy. It was pouring rain and I stood under the awning of the café watching the water hit the ground. We had this amazing conversation and I could see the Festival coming to life right in front of my eyes. It was such a powerful feeling. Drew was funny, engaging and very relatable. We had spoken about what role Drew might enjoy and after telling him what our needs were, I asked him to draw up his own job description. We continued to work with his role and ended up deciding that he would manage the Festival's relationships with different studios around town, in addition to generally helping the team wherever we needed it.

Kurt also connected us with Courtney, someone else he knew in the scene. He only had the most wonderful things to say about Courtney. Originally we had connected over email but I forgot to respond to a message from Courtney and the connection went dormant. Conscious Counsel was in its incipient months and I was focusing more of my time on the law firm. So, when I received a follow-up email from Courtney a few months later (persistence – such an important quality), I was thrilled to connect. When I look back on how everything unfolded, I can't help but think how different MYF would have been if Courtney had not followed up. So, THANK YOU Courtney for doing so.

My first conversation with Courtney was different than the ones I'd had with Drew and Kurt. Courtney has a much softer personality, and until you get to know her you might mistake this for timidity. But now that I know Courtney well, I think she just does a great job of listening and giving others space to share what they need to share. We spoke on the phone and it was clear that there was a perfect fit for her and the Festival. In addition, I got my first glimpses of how special Courtney is. She is very passionate and committed to helping and serving others. She was especially passionate about our values of Community, Connection and Conservation, and had lots of experience as an entrepreneur and volunteer. These would be very valuable assets for MYF. We decided Courtney would start off helping with our online presence and organizing Festival volunteers, and then go forward from there.

So, this was how it started. This was our band. If you came to the Festival, this is who you have to thank for an amazing weekend: Courtney, Drew, Kurt and Ashley Boone. This was the team that dreamed up and created the Muskoka Yoga Festival. Trust me when I say that we couldn't have done as amazing a job as we did without this team.

If you are trying to create anything new, build a team. It makes everything more fun, allows you to crosscheck all of your ideas and brings fresh perspectives to the table. The reach of what you can accomplish is extended infinitely when you bring capable and positive people onto your team. When I look back to the Muskoka Yoga Festival, I can tell you that it would not have been possible without the help of our team. No way. I couldn't have done it without Ashley. Ashley and I couldn't have done it without Kurt. And, Ashley, Kurt and I couldn't have done it without Courtney and Drew. Get the picture? Power in numbers, all the way.

The Importance of Having Clear Contracts

Throughout this whole book, I've constantly been harping on the need for clear and honest communication in your working relationships. It is the basic foundation on which everything is built upon. When you create clear agreements with your team, you can state your expectations of the team and also set specific goals that you seek to accomplish. If team members aren't doing something or you aren't doing something, you can easily return to the agreement to show what needs aren't being met and change course accordingly.

Concise and specific agreements set the road for successful relationships – and I learned this lesson the hard way. The truth is that we didn't have agreements signed with our three key team members and that hurt us. A lot. Muskoka Yoga Festival was really my first experience being a manager and I knew nothing about how to do it. It was also my first time putting on any event, not to mention a big-scale yoga festival, and I knew nothing about how to do that either. It was trial by fire in its most authentic application.

The reason we didn't have agreements with our team was mostly because there were so many *uncertainties* about what would happen with the Festival. Would it even happen? How much would we be in debt? Would anyone show up? We had no idea what was going on, and even though we were having a blast talking about this Festival, we had no proof that it would actually happen. Was it all a big dream?

One of the major uncertainties in our organization came

from the lack of clear outlines for what each individual's responsibilities would be. We'd start working on what someone's role looked like, but then out of nowhere we'd need their help in another area we hadn't thought about yet. Suddenly, that person was stepping in to do something that we previously didn't even know needed to be done. It was a constant scramble. It was my fault and I take full responsibility for it. My defense is that I had no idea what I was doing, but I know that isn't good enough. We're always learning.

In addition to the constantly shifting demands on our team, we didn't have any money to pay our team. Since we had no idea if we'd make any money, we also didn't know if we'd be able to pay them. This wasn't as bad as you might think, because we told everyone that the Festival was a start-up and that no one gets paid when the business is fighting for survival. The deal was that if we were in the red, we wouldn't be able to pay anyone and all of their efforts would be in the name of community. Everyone was cool with that. But if we were profitable (an idea so fanciful in the months leading up to the Festival), it wasn't clear exactly how much our team would get paid, but we would try our best.

There were so many things going on at one moment and we were so distracted by trying to actually do this thing that we never really made time to sit down and say, "Okay, this is how it is going to work." In hindsight, I can rationalize and understand *why* this happened but I still wish it could have happened differently and with more structure. I loved our family the most. If we put on a great festival for our community but didn't empower the people who really helped build it, honouring them with a feeling of dignity and respect, then it would be a fail. So, I failed. In the end, we survived (yippee!) and were able to pay everyone on our team. But I would have liked for all the relationships to have had a bit more structure.

The lesson I learned through this experience is that even though all of the logistics and demands of putting on a major event can be chaotic and distracting, it is important to solidify your relationships with the people who matter upfront. The point is that *I hated the feeling that I could have done more to instil a sense of respect in our relationships with the people who matter most.* We could have communicated our expectations of them and let them communicate their expectations to us. If you are wondering why I constantly harp on the importance of radical honesty and structure to relationships, it is because I personally know what it is like to let down people I love. I don't want anyone to have to go through that. The lesson: Memorialize the working relationships you have with your team. This has to be your top priority.

The Moment Everything Changed

There was one pivotal moment where the momentum of the Festival changed – and it proved to be one the greatest lessons I've ever learned. We had a team meeting somewhere in Yorkville to prepare for our Toronto launch party, which was to take place in a few days at The Local on Ossington Avenue. We were just starting the month of April, meaning we had three months to go and ticket sales, from my perspective, were abysmal. I think we had sold twenty-something tickets, most of which had gone to personal friends. At this point, I was convinced that no one was going to show up to the Festival.

During the meeting, I was harping on the need for us to sell tickets to anyone who came to the event. It was a fear-driven approach, brought on by my doubts that we could survive. The team must have thought I was nuts. Ashley was much calmer and the voice of reason, as she always is. "Let's try our best and make sure we let people know what we are about," she said reassuringly. "God, what would I do without her?" I thought to myself.

That afternoon I went for a workout at Equinox and met Kurt afterwards to chat. At this point, we were bros and Kurt has a great ability to be direct and say what is on his mind. "Bro," he started, "I'm a bit worried after today's meeting. It felt like there was an energy of anxiety around the meeting." He was so right. I had brought my anxiety to the team and spread it across the whole team. "Ticket sales will come," he continued, "but let's just focus on having a calm and relaxing space to build this for others." And that was it. Kurt was right. Kurt was so right. From that moment on, I NEVER checked our ticket sales. Not once. All I did was focus my energy on making sure there was a calm and relaxing space around the team. I always measured the energy I was bringing to the team and made sure that no aspect of it was negative.

There are two layers of significance to this story – and both proved to be transformative for my life and career. The first is that this moment was *a microcosm for the incredibly unique skill set that yogis bring to the table in business.* They are special. They may not know about legal agreements, but what they do know is invaluable. A big reason why I am drawn to working in yoga and with yogis is the amazing people and how different it is to work with them compared to the rest of the world. The second thing I learned from this was *the importance of intentions in the actions you take.* I was able to shift all of my energy away from thinking about how many tickets we'd sell and if anyone would show, and instead concentrate on just having fun, loosening up and focusing on what we could control. I knew we could control the energy around our meetings and made it my prerogative to always keep things fresh and fun.

The day of our event at The Local, I told the team that we weren't going to sell any tickets. Instead, we'd just make sure everyone had a good time. They definitely thought I was nuts, but that wasn't anything new. The event went off without a hitch and I think we had about 25 people show. The date was April 1, 2017 and it was as auspicious a date as could be. The afternoon of the gathering, my sister Lauren had given birth to her first child, sweet Raffi Shane. Raff is the first grandchild to my parents and my first nephew. Our family was growing. And as I stood on top of the bar at our first Muskoka Yoga Festival event since building our team, looking down at all of these new faces, I saw another kind of growth. I invited everyone to raise their glasses and welcomed them to our family. Expansion was ever present. This was actually happening.

Turning Air into Reality

One of the most fascinating parts of putting on a yoga festival that didn't yet exist was realizing how much of the festival existed in our words. Actually, until the gates to the park opened up on July 7, 2017, the entire Festival was just one massive grouping of air. When you are selling a product that doesn't exist, all that you can do is tell people about it. You get used to telling so many people about it that somehow it becomes real. But if we wanted to tell people to save a summer weekend and book transportation and accommodation ninety minutes from where we lived, we had to show them *something*. Words and air can only go so far.

And so, I believe that one of the best things we did to spread the word about the Festival was to create a promotional video. We wanted to showcase the beautiful land where the Festival would take place and interview a few of our teachers to show what we were about. I believed that if we could give the Festival a voice and video footage, it would resonate. (I have no idea if this premonition was correct — one frustrating thing about putting on an event is that you don't really know what worked and what didn't work.)

Our video was shot by none other than the immensely talented and incredibly kind Darko Sikman, a friend of mine from Vancouver. He flew out to Toronto and chilled with me for seventy-two hours straight, as we huffed it from the city to Muskoka and back. The guy is an artistic genius and an absolute workhorse. Our whole team was so thrilled with the final product. Darko was in Ontario for a total of three jam-packed days, two of which involved red-eye flights. When a friend helps you out like that, you never forget it. I include this part of the story to highlight the importance of *appreciating the right people* when you find them.

We loved the video and invested a bit of money to promote it online. Suddenly, when I would talk to potential sponsors or interested vendors, I had something to show them other than a link to our website and their response was always positive. Again, while I can't be certain that the video contributed to a solid showing at the Festival, I think it contributed positively.

I have also included this little story about the promotional video because I want to touch on the legal issues that arise when you record a video or take photographs. There are two distinct relationships involved in creating a movie or taking photographs, and each one raises important issues that you need to be aware of:

- *Relationship 1:* Your relationship with the person who makes the video or shoots the photographs. Issue: Who owns the rights to the video? Are the rights shared? Or in addition to purchasing the video, are you purchasing ownership to the content in the video?
- *Relationship 2:* Your relationship with the people who are shown in the video or the photographs. Issue: Have you obtained the proper permission from them to use their image/video/likeness however you'd like and for as long as you'd like? Have you taken the appropriate measures to check if you are using the image/likeness of a minor, and if so, have you obtained permission to do so from the minor's guardian?

Finally, I have included the story about our promotional video to *encourage anyone putting on an event (especially if it has never happened) to make a video for it.* Just think about how much more enticed you would be to go on a retreat or attend a festival if you could actually see what it would look like. The litmus test for making a decision is always thinking about how you would behave – and after Ash and I watched beautiful videos of other festivals and found ourselves wanting to go, we knew that we needed to create our own video. Paint a picture for people and lead their imagination. Make it easier for them to join you on your journey.

Your Chapter Checklist:

- If you want to put on a yoga event or festival, first ask yourself "why" and let that be your compass for the decisions you make.
- Having a strong team will empower you to achieve more in less time and have fun doing so.

- Whatever you are doing, be sure to believe in it all the way. No one may show up at the start, but stay true to yourself and your vision and you can create anything. Never doubt but always check-in with yourself.
- Bringing an energy of calmness and lightness to facilitating a big event goes a long way instead of stress and anxiety. Do your best to surround your tribe with positive vibes.

Chapter 10

Savasana: Lessons + Results from the Yoga Festival

Intention

With a team, I have taken a yoga festival from ideation to full-blown execution, and I am hoping to share the lessons I've learned from the experience so that others don't make the same mistakes I did. It is worth mentioning that these lessons can apply to other events too. Yoga festivals are similar to other sorts of festivals – music festivals, food festivals, religious festivals, etc. – but they differentiate themselves in being centered around, not surprisingly, yoga! Even within the broad category of "yoga festival," there are many different types of events. Some will offer only yoga classes and workshops, while others will have a range of events in which yoga is just a small component. Some may align perfectly with what you are looking for and others may be everything you wish didn't exist. It doesn't matter! What matters is that it is inspiring that people make the effort to create a community they believe will make a positive change in the world.

If you remember only one thing from this chapter, remember that if there is a type of festival or event that you think should exist but does not yet exist... well... share your gift with the world! Part of why I wrote this book is to tell true stories of people who just decided to go for it and do things – and in the end made a difference. So if you are scratching your head at this moment thinking, "What about that great idea I had…" a lawyer has told you to just go for it!

A Million Little Relationships

Remember in the first chapter when I asked you to make a page that captured all of your relationships, including all the different categories and sub-categories? When I did the same exercise for the Muskoka Yoga Festival, I literally had to use three pieces of paper. There are so many relationships going on when you plan a major event that it can make your head spin. Just by way of example, you have relationships with:

- The municipality of the town where you organize the event;
- The vendors;
- The insurance company that supplies the policy for the event;
- The attendees (the clients!);
- The musicians;
- The venue;
- The teachers;
- The volunteers;
- The sponsors;
- The staff;
- The ground crew who set up the venue;
- The food trucks;
- The beverage tent;
- The charity organization you donate profits to;
- The accommodation venues to host your people;
- The transportation companies to drop off and pick up everything on time;

- The government grants that support you.

The list goes on, but I'll save both of us time and let the above suffice. When you break all of these different categories into smaller categories, you really get to see how many different relationships you have when you put on a major event. When I look back on the experience, I think we did a great job of organizing most of these working relationships, especially having never done anything like this before. But I did learn a few things through the experience that I'd like to share with you, so you don't have to make the same mistakes we made.

I will succinctly summarize all of these lessons, but as I do so, I just want to remind you of the important lesson at hand. If we had said what we really felt at the time of entering into all of these relationships and recorded our expectations in writing, none of these issues would have happened. These are just examples of *how things can go poorly if you don't memorialize agreements properly when you make them.*

Here some examples of where things went pear-shaped for us because we didn't lock up our agreements properly.

Lesson 1: The Sponsor Who Did Not Want to Pay

For weeks leading up to the Festival, we had been in talks with a sponsor and finally came to an agreement. We agreed that they would be the exclusive sponsor for a particular category, and that in return they would execute an activation at the festival. We agreed to the price they would pay and everything seemed sorted. At that point, we stopped looking for sponsors in that particular category. Wouldn't you know that only three days before the event, after we had done everything to accommodate their activation, the sponsor told us that they wouldn't be paying us. They could do their activation for free but they couldn't pay us the agreed upon amount. *This was a very sneaky and unprofessional move.* They basically waited until the last second to pigeonhole us where we'd have no other options and then pull out from paying. We learned a lot from this experience, chiefly that this is just the way that some companies do business. While you'd hope that everyone acts with integrity and honesty, this isn't always the case. We are lucky that we learned this important lesson with such minimal damage. Obviously, we'll never do business with those people again.

Lesson Learned: Get people to commit to their promises in writing, otherwise they may try to wiggle their way out of them.

Lesson 2: When Will We Ever Get Paid?

We had an awesome working relationship with a not-for-profit organization that helped local businesses in Muskoka get off the ground. They were super supportive of our initiatives and were very helpful in assisting us with some really important things, especially as we were just getting going. We had sent them a proposal for different projects that we needed help funding, including rough numbers for each idea, and they agreed to help cover the costs. *What we didn't specify with enough detail was exactly how much each item would cost, or when they would pay us back.* So off we went with our credit cards to pay for things believing that we would be reimbursed. They weren't necessarily things we would have paid for out of our own pockets, but since we had a partner who wanted to help, getting these things done was a value-added bonus.

As you might imagine, there was a lot of confusion when it came to getting paid back for the costs we had incurred.

The first part of the battle was outlining what they had agreed to pay and for what. The second part was establishing when they would pay us. *The problem here is that when you don't make agreements with enough specificity, you are at a significant risk of loss.* The process of dealing with an organization we loved in this way was challenging, because we had to be firm even though they had been such a big help to us. But up to that point, they hadn't paid for anything and hadn't even been a help. They were in total control of the situation. If they didn't want to pay us, they didn't really have to. Our oral agreements were vague enough that they could have gotten out of it if they had wanted. Plus, we needed cash to pay all of our expenses. In the end, after we had waited a few months, they eventually did pay for everything they'd said they would – but I vowed that I would never again be in such a vulnerable position.

Lesson Learned: Outline how much you will get paid and when you will get paid when you are building relationships with partners. Get it down in writing so that you have something to point to should the process stall. Leave nothing in ambiguity or uncertainty.

Lesson 3: Unclear Teacher Agreements

A common mistake that a lot of new business operators make is that *they want everyone to like them.* Often, they'll let things slide or let themselves be taken advantage of because they want all the different people they work with to like them. It is human, after all, to want to be liked and accepted by others. How much more so for a brand-new event that has the ideals of connection and community as its foundation. We encountered a bit of a difficulty with some teachers who had invited their friends to help co-teach their classes. The problem was that they were expecting us to pay their friends the same amount we were paying them to teach the class, in addition to giving their friends weekend passes and the other perks of being MYF teachers. While we had teacher agreements, the agreements didn't explicitly state whether or not teachers could bring friends, and whether or not such friends would be compensated. All of this came to a head as the teachers were driving up to Muskoka. When we asked them about these arrangements, they told us that they had been cleared through someone on our team. Here, again, we saw the need for organization and specific roles within a team. In the end, we did not protest and were happy to welcome everyone to teach at our festival. But it was clear that there was a miscommunication and that all of it was my fault.

Lesson Learned: Outline exactly what teachers can and cannot do, and what you will and will not pay for. Do this from the start to ensure that there are no surprises at the last second.

Lesson 4: The Independent Contractor Who Lasted One Day

We needed help in the entertainment department because Ashley and I had no experience with booking talent to play any sort of shows. We got connected with a dude who came highly recommended by someone Ashley knew, and then we sort of rushed into one of those unclear, ambiguous, handshake-solidifying type of working arrangements. It took roughly twenty-four hours to see that there wasn't a fit in working together, and suddenly our concerns shifted from putting on a great event to finding a way out of this relationship. Worst of all, this guy was under the impression that he was entitled to a $1,000 signing bonus just for agreeing to work with us. There were probably four or five days when this issue clouded our work until we came clean, communicated openly and honestly, and told the IC that we had to go our separate ways. It ended okay but Ashley and I were not pleased that someone was dissatisfied working with us.

Lesson Learned: Be clear about all aspects of a relationship from beginning to end before you agree to work with someone.

The First Muskoka Yoga Festival

The first Muskoka Yoga Festival was a stunning success – mostly because it actually happened. Having had many ideas in my life that never materialized, or found a way to flake before actualization, I think I was most proud that the Festival actually took place. I know that it never could have happened without Ashley, our families and our amazing team.

On the Friday night of the Festival, we had a lovely gathering at a local food market with music, drinks and light bites. It was so much fun to be with all of these people and incredibly fulfilling to know that our team had facilitated this experience. I was able to put faces to names that I had only seen in my email inbox before. I was so glad to be surrounded by such wonderful people. I realized that there wasn't anything especially different about organizing a festival compared with attending a festival, and once this fact hit me – that I was at a yoga festival – I jumped right in and had the best time.

It is difficult to describe the emotional experience and release of planning and talking about an idea for months on end, unsure if it will succeed or flop or be a disaster or be incredible, and then finally being in it. Festival weekend flew by and I only remember three things from the whole weekend:

1. The moment the first classes started and the Festival

was actually happening. I looked out onto the field where the Festival was taking place while chatting with Kurt. "People actually showed up," I said, almost in disbelief. "Yeah they did. Oh, and look at how many people are at Rachel Fallon's class taking place right now; it's overflowing from the tent. I'm just living for her right now." We made eye contact, burst out into laughter and shared a hug.

2. After the first day of yoga programming was over, I remember joining Ashley for a beer in the little beer garden and laughing together in the sunshine. It was a very special moment – to look at how all of our hard work had culminated in bringing these people together. We clinked our beer cans together with big smiles, and then had the best time jumping and dancing to reggae music at a free concert we put on for our community.

3. The last thing I remember about the Festival is it being over. We cleaned up the site on Sunday afternoon and then I returned to my parents' place to take a shower. I parked my car, exhaled loudly and walked to the door. As I entered through the side, I caught my dad taking a small nap on the couch, watching golf. The moment he saw me, he stood up and with a big smile gave me a standing round of applause. I motioned him to stop and sit down, but he kept going. Without saying it, we were both thinking of that night where two people showed up and how hard we had worked to have over three hundred in Muskoka for the Festival. For that moment alone, it was all worth it. We had put on a yoga festival.

Improvements in the Second Year

Without a doubt, putting on a festival is much easier in the second year than the first. The first year we really had no idea what we were doing. Heading into the second year, we still had no idea what we were doing except that we knew we could do it – and we had a few ideas about what didn't work during the first year. The tricky thing about putting on an event for the second time is that you have some form of expectation for putting it on, which you never had in the first place because you hadn't known what to expect.

On a personal level, Ashley and I had both decided to go travelling for the year. I had decided to take Conscious Counsel online and fulfil a lifelong dream to spend three months in India. Ashley had followed the waves of her heart to pursue a life in which she could surf as much as physically possible in Bali, Thailand and Sri Lanka. Without any plan whatsoever, we decided to build the Festival again from all around the world. While this was happening, our team was based in Toronto helping us on the ground.

In hindsight, I failed miserably as a manager (or should I say that I learned a lot?) because I didn't take the distances into account in our relationships. And just as we didn't have clear agreements in place with our team for the first year of the Festival, we didn't really address the issue of distance and things remained unclear. I really lacked a sense of professionalism. At the core, we continued to run the Festival like a passion project with our friends, except that now we were asking them to actually do things for the Festival year round. This resulted in a lot of challenges and regrettably strained our relationships with people we really cared for.

I share this information only in the hope that you (or

others) will not make the same mistakes that I did when leading a team. Losing the friends I worked with because of professional differences or a lack of structure on my end, especially people who had contributed so lovingly to an amazing community event, is one of the regrets of my life (I don't have many) although I know I have become better for it. I cannot over-stress the importance of putting strict guidelines on role definitions and expectations for the people you work with. This allows everyone to feel comfortable, valued and aligned with the purpose of the organization.

However, for our second year, we started fresh with a new team and had very specific agreements with all of them. This was beneficial for everyone – the Festival, our team and everyone we worked with. We consistently held team meetings, worked hard to increase our presence in the community and created fun initiatives for our second festival. We decided to have a boat cruise on the Friday night and had an ecstatic dance party on the Saturday night. Most importantly, *we began to put in place systems and processes* for our business that were instrumental to our professionalization (and growing up). Oh yeah, and we started to treat our Festival like a business, which also took some mental evolution.

The second Muskoka Yoga Festival was an incredible success. All of our numbers doubled from the first year to the second year, but more importantly, people had the best time. The most consistent feedback we got from the Festival was that it had a great and relaxed energy, which was a product of our amazing team and instructors. People were hanging out by the river, jumping and dancing covered in paint, and connected with nature and themselves. At the end of the Festival, our team had a massive team hug and it was clear that we had impacted the lives of many for the better – and truly created a community.

Once again, time passed by so quickly at the Festival that I am reduced to two singular memories from the entire experience:

1. The feeling that the Saturday of the Festival was one of the best days of my life. I remember pulling out of the Patterson Kaye Lodge (our 2018 MYF Retreat Sponsor) after a sing-along circle by the beach, feeling so immensely proud of Ashley and myself for bringing so many people together in such a beautiful way. This day was one of the FUNNEST days of my life.

2. Our team's group hug to close out the Festival. We were all so happy and proud. We had a team debrief and then hugged it out together. We had worked tirelessly and invested a ton of energy, but the end product was incredibly fulfilling. We did it.

Reflections Entering Our Third Year

There were many transitions in our Festival from the end of the second year to the start of the third. At the 2018 Festival, a few of our team members conducted surveys and we gleaned a lot of information from the feedback. *I would highly recommend that anyone running a business listen to their customers as much as possible.* We were thrilled that people loved our event so much, but we also took their suggestions to heart. When you put on a festival and are taking people's time and money, you have an obligation to give them the best experience possible.

From an administrative point of view, Ashley and I needed to take a big pause in our relationship and ask ourselves why we were doing this. We started this initiative to create community, connection and raise awareness for conservation. Had we done this? If so, what was next? After two years, you have to ask yourself *why* and *how* you are doing certain things.

What I found in my self-explorations was that I had never been more excited to work on the Festival. We were gaining momentum, put down roots in a community and were faced with incredible potential. I was adamant on finding a venue with camping, knowing that this would contribute greatly to the experience. We had learned a ton about online marketing after working with Seymour Wood, an internet and marketing guru, and felt we could reach our audience and communicate our message to them like never before. I felt we were so close to offering the true festival experience I had always wanted to facilitate for others.

We are still in the early days of the third year, but already we are eons above and beyond where we were in the past. In the first year, you have no idea what you are doing. In the second year, you have a slight idea and try the same things twice, to see which ones actually work. In the third year, I feel that you know what works and you do more of it.

The single most important lesson I've learned in the third year of the Festival is: Only work with professionals. The new test we have for anyone joining our team is, *"is this what they do for a living?"* When you treat a business like a business, you need professionals. We loved having help from anyone who would offer it, but at the end of the day you need professionals running your business in order to achieve professional goals. That has been the big lesson of planning Muskoka Yoga Festival in its third year.

That being said, heading into the third year of something that was once just a dream, I want to conclude the Muskoka Yoga Festival story by sharing two sentiments that will apply to you if you are running a yoga business or event:

1. Patience is paramount. This applies to life and business

and organizing yoga events. Life as an entrepreneur means accepting that you probably won't get paid for years, if at all. This is why the second point matters so much...

2. Passion is the most important ingredient for facilitating an event. If you don't love doing it, others won't love your event. You'll get tired and angry and frustrated if you aren't doing it because you love it. If you love it, you'll see there is nothing else you could possibly do, and that is why you continue to do it.

Final Thoughts

DO IT. Just do it. If you have an idea or an event or something your heart has always been calling you to do, just go for it. Even if you fail miserably and lose all of your money, it will be the best thing you ever did in your life. You'll grow, you'll learn and the Universe will reward you for trying to make the world a better place. As human beings, we have an obligation to try to make all of our lives better, even if it's only for an hour-long yoga class or a weekend festival. Be the change. Lead with your heart. Try your best.

Your Chapter Checklist:

*   Do everything possible to have all of your relationships set out as clearly as possible before starting to work with someone in any capacity. Think of the possible questions or uncertainties (i.e. when will we get paid) in the relationship and tackle them head on.
*   Appreciate the vast number of relationships you'll have in facilitating an event, break them down as best as

possible and communicate expectations within each of them.

- You should only be putting on your event if it lights you up and you have a zealous passion for it. This enthusiasm and drive will be the prana for you, your team and your community.
- Do it. Whatever it is you've ever wanted to do, DO IT. You'll succeed or fail, but in the end we are alive to pursue our passions and make a difference. You learn from every experience, so take the leap. It is always worth it.

About the Author

Cory Sterling completed a yoga teacher training in Nasik, India in 2017 after practicing (and loving) yoga for five years. Yoga served as the catalyst for Cory's first glimpses of awareness and meditation, which have changed his life. He has been a lawyer since 2015 and started his own law firm, Conscious Counsel, in 2017. He co-founded the Muskoka Yoga Festival in 2016, which takes place in Muskoka, Ontario every July. He has always aspired to be an author, having written many travel stories during his adventures abroad, but he never, ever would have believed that his first book would be about Yoga Law. Accepting and embracing the Universe, he is thrilled with how everything has worked out.

More About the Author

Yoga Legal, powered by Conscious Counsel Legal Services was established in 2016 to make working with the law FUN for yogis. By drafting agreements with a main ingredient of LOVE, approaching legal issues with compassion and protecting your yoga business mindfully, Yoga Legal has transformed the way legal services are offered for yoga professionals.

Website: www.yogalegal.com
Instagram: @consciouscounsel

Disclaimer: The content in this book IS NOT LEGAL advice and by you purchasing this book, NO LAWYER-CLIENT RELATIONSHIP is created between us. I am simply sharing my practical understanding of the law as I've experienced it in my own legal practice and in working with my clients. You are fully responsible for any actions you take or do not take based on the information in this book and release the author and Conscious Counsel Legal Services from any liability as a result of your reading this book. Thanks for understanding this!